BERKLEE PRESS

THE PRACTICAL JAZZ GUITARIST

essential tools for soloing, comping, and performing

MARK WHITE

Edited by Jonathan Feist

Berklee Press

Vice President of Berklee Media: David Kusek
Vice President of Berklee Media: Debbie Cavalier
Assistant Vice President/CFO of Berklee Media: Robert F. Green
Managing Editor: Jonathan Feist
Editorial Assistants: Jimmy Haas, David Hume, Ben Scudder, Jacqueline Sim, Won (Sara) Hwang
Cover Designer: Kathy Kikkert
Cover Photograph: Judah Chivian

ISBN 978-0-87639-124-2

DISTRIBUTED BY

HAL•LEONARD®
CORPORATION

1140 Boylston Street
Boston, MA 02215-3693 USA
(617) 747-2146

Visit Berklee Press Online at
www.berkleepress.com

7777 W. BLUEMOUND RD. P.O. BOX 13819
MILWAUKEE, WISCONSIN 53213

Visit Hal Leonard Online at
www.halleonard.com

CONTENTS

CD TRACKS

ABOUT THE RECORDING

Mark White: Guitars

Scott deOgburn: Fender Rhodes Piano

Bill Miele: Bass

Kenny Hadley: Drums

Recorded, mixed, and mastered by Mark White at Gorgon Studio

ACKNOWLEDGMENTS

A great deal of praise and thanks are due to the many people involved in the preparation of this book. Let me start with Susanna Chivian, who edited the original manuscript and made suggestions that added to the cohesiveness and readability of this book. To Larry Baione, chair of the Berklee Guitar Department for his reviewing the materials and support of the project. To Jonathan Feist, managing editor at Berklee Press, for the great expertise, ideas, and down-to-earth humor that have helped the project come together. To Kelly Belinsky, MS, OTR/L, for reviewing and suggestions on the hand health information. To Damian Bracken, head of admissions at Berklee, for his interview in appendix B. To Kenny Hadley (drums), Bill Miele (bass), and Scott deOgburn (keyboards), who were the musicians that played the examples on the CD. All these musicians are longtime friends and world-class and first-call players with whom I've traveled the world. Thank you for bringing your great talents to this project!

Additional thanks are owed to Scott deOgburn who helped me proof all the musical examples. Thanks are due also to the wonderful guitarist and musician Johnny Smith for confirmation of his tuning method, and to Antonio Mendoza for his virtuoso guitar artistry, expertise, and support. In remembrance of the late cellist Bernard Greenhouse for his visionary insight on music, technique, and performance. He truly was a musical titan. To all the marvelous musicians and teachers who have helped me over the years, and to the support staff at Berklee Press and to Hal Leonard for their committed work on this book.

This book is dedicated to Joe Pass, who was such an inspiring teacher in my early years. I still use many ideas in my playing and teaching that he passed on to me. And to Charlie Banacos, who was my longtime mentor, a wonderful human being, and the finest musician that I have ever known. Charlie had a profound musical effect on musicians all over the planet. He will always be remembered.

INTRODUCTION

Making It Real

MAKING PROGRESS

Learning to play jazz guitar is a challenging and time-consuming enterprise, as well as a very rewarding one. There are many approaches presented out there in the market, and there is a lot of great material to consider while you're learning. One piece of advice I'd like to offer: **Make it real!**

In order to advance quickly, it is important to be grounded in musical reality. Musicians often get swept off course by too much information and not enough practical application—that is, playing. Swayed by diverse methods of technique and a myriad of theoretical information, we all yo-yo back and forth in our day-to-day quest to become better guitarists. We're tempted by quick fixes. Videos, online lessons, and the river of information available on the Internet are all informative but often overwhelming at the same time. Beware of the "flavor of the day" mentality. Consistency of approach, steady, regular practice, and application of materials incorporated into tunes (i.e., music making) is the way to go.

I view the musical learning experience as being a three-stage process:

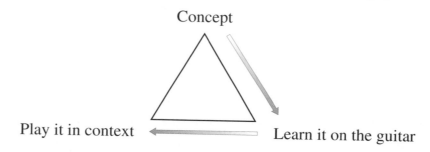

Fig. I.1. Music Learning Triangle

The three corners of the learning triangle could be described as:

1. **Concept.** Learn an improved device, such as chord outlining for soloing.

2. **Learn it on the guitar.** This is the doing stage. Find fingerings, develop lines, play in twelve keys, etc.

3. **Play it in context.** Learn to fit these lines into a jazz tune, work on phrasing, time, and articulation, etc. This is the real-life application of a concept, and the crucial step that many never quite reach.

Being able to take an idea from the concept stage to using it while playing in a musical context is the goal here. The ability to use an idea in a solo or within a groove is what separates the "players" from the students. Make it real!

A wonderful example of someone with this mentality would be Wes Montgomery. Completely self-taught on guitar, Wes couldn't read music and had little concept of musical theory. He became one of the greatest jazz guitarists of all time by learning things grounded in musical reality. Starting by copying Charlie Christian's guitar solos by ear, Wes developed a groundbreaking concept of location, fingering, and phrasing of these ideas on the fingerboard. He also created a unique, right-hand technique that embodied the quality of sound (tone quality) that he imagined by using his thumb instead of using a pick. Initially, Wes played the Christian solos verbatim with a local group, but then he learned how to develop his own improvising vocabulary, incorporating from Charlie Parker and the bop giants of the day. He gained experience through gigging with other musicians. His performance experiences developed his harmonic knowledge and comping, taught him jazz repertoire, and influenced his own compositions, which are still played by jazz musicians across the globe. You could rephrase it like this: Get a concept together, figure out the best way to play it on your instrument, then play it on a tune on the gig. This is the way practical guitarists learn their craft.

Certainly, times have changed since Wes was out there cookin' up a storm. He's still a great model and a hero, but the logistics of making a living in music have changed since his time, and practical jazz guitarists need to be diverse in their musical skills nowadays. A very fortunate few perform and record only, but the typical contemporary jazz guitarist is a great performer, reads well, is stylistically diverse, is knowledgeable about the tradition of the guitar in jazz, and teaches professionally. We do jazz gigs, travel to perform at festivals, and often teach clinics at these festivals. In addition to our jazz activities, we do studio work, playing in a variety of idioms. We play Broadway shows and do theater work. Our teaching posts at music schools and colleges incorporate teaching playing skills, as well as musicianship skills like sight-reading and ear training.

So, while the lion's share of this book is dedicated to developing the art of jazz guitar in practical ways that are playing oriented, you'll also find information about becoming a well-rounded musician, how to develop sight-reading skills on the guitar, and preparing auditions for professional music schools. It is my hope that you will find the information contained here to be substantial, engaging, and *practical* in your study of the jazz guitar!

Mark White
March 2, 2011, Boston

PART I

YOUR TOOLKIT

CHAPTER 1

The Basic Toolkit

PLAYING ERGONOMICS AND HAND HEALTH

Before starting out on a serious study of jazz guitar, it makes sense to look at how the mechanics of guitar technique work. I have two primary objectives in mind here: first, to establish a technique that doesn't hinder performance, and second, to ensure long-term hand health, to help you avoid injuries like tendonitis, carpal tunnel syndrome, and other nerve compression-related injuries. There is a great deal of variance in personal technique among all great guitarists. This can be due to individual physical characteristics, as well as to the stylistic traits, of a player, e.g., playing fingerstyle or with a pick or thumb, and articulated picking vs. legato style playing, for instance.

One thing all great players have in common: they've got to work with Mother Nature to play what they've got to say! Regardless of whether you are a burning virtuoso or an introspective technical minimalist, you have to use your natural tools effectively in order to progress rapidly on the guitar. And of course, we want to be playing for a long, healthy time over a long career. When you see a great guitarist perform who seems to make his playing look effortless, you are witnessing a good working technique. But when a player "makes it look easy," there's been a lot of time invested in honing that technique. Playing experience obviously has an important role in technical development.

WHERE TO START

A good place to begin learning about how to play guitar is by observing great players. In addition to checking out live performers, there is a gigantic amount of instructional and performance video available. We can gain oceans of knowledge just by observing these films.

Start by looking at how great players hold their instruments. There's a lot of range here. Are we looking at someone playing a Fender Telecaster or a Gibson L5? If you are watching a video of Wes Montgomery playing, notice how he holds the lower bout of the instrument away from his body. He also uses a strap. The positioning of his guitar allowed Wes to play with a "natural" posture that aided his technique.

Don't limit yourself to just watching jazz guitarists. Wonderful film footage of classical guitarists like John Williams and Andrés Segovia, or fusion players like Frank Gambale and Scott Henderson, are just a click away on your computer. Learn by watching and listening. A super-technician like those mentioned have reached a supreme level of ergonomics through years of experience practicing and performing. Imitate the way your favorite guitarists hold their instruments and see if it feels like a good fit for you. Look at their hands, and how the guitar interfaces with their body.

That being said, there are some basic guidelines that can help you get your technique together. Start from what's known as "at rest position." Sit in a chair, and without the guitar, observe how your shoulders are level on both sides. Your upper body is relaxed without jutting a shoulder forward, and your arms should hang freely at your sides. Now, pick up the guitar and place it so as to maintain this "at rest position." You might need a strap, or perhaps you play classical fingerstyle with nylon strings and use a footstool or a lap baluster to obtain this positioning. If you stand when you play, adapt the "at rest position" from a walking position: one foot in front of the other, with your upper body relaxed. Now bring your arms up on the guitar. Both arms should interface with the guitar in a comfortable and "natural" way. See how it looks in a mirror. Adjust how you hold the instrument so things feel comfortable for you. Everyone is built differently and there's room for customizing these guidelines.

Once you've got the basic positioning, look at some general technique guidelines for each hand. Regardless of whether you play right- or left-handed, your fingering hand should hold the guitar neck loosely, with just enough pressure between the thumb and fingers to play notes and chords clearly, but not too much pressure from overexerting. Try to keep the wrist fairly straight. Remember: *this is only a guideline*! Location and execution of some ideas on the fingerboard will necessitate bending the wrist. To get this positioning picture in your head, drop your fingering hand to your side. You'll notice that the wrist is straight and your hand is loose. Transfer this image to the guitar neck. Howard Roberts described it (in his excellent book, *Howard Roberts Guitar Manual*, Cherry Lane 1972) as like picking up a broomstick, with your wrist straight, your fingers slightly curled, your thumb pointing towards the headstock, and your hand cradling the neck loosely.

What we're trying to achieve here is comfortable positioning for the fingering hand that enhances performance ergonomics and promotes healthy technique. Chronic overexertion can lead to tendonitis, and chronically bad wrist posture can cause carpal tunnel and other nerve compression-related issues. Keep in mind that the broomstick concept pertains mainly to executing "scalar" passages. Flattening the fingers and rolling across adjacent strings to execute intervals and arpeggios is good too. Just don't overemphasize the motion or grip too hard.

Of all the issues concerning guitar technique, none are more diverse in conception than the "picking" hand's posture. Using a pick, playing finger-style—there are myriad techniques that can vary dramatically from player to player. "Picking" hand technique has a lot to do with a players phrasing and idea-location conception. Some guitarists have what I call an "articulated" picking technique. Players such as Pat Martino and John McLaughlin come to mind. They pick a great many of the notes they play. Other players, such as Pat Metheny or Jim Hall, utilize more of a legato technique that incorporates extensive use of slurs and hammer-ons. All players use elements of both these techniques to shape their phrasing and to execute their ideas. This is a good time to observe some of your favorite players again (videos, live performances) for a place to start.

After you get an idea of how you want to start posture-wise, drop the picking hand to your side and let your hand relax. Bring the hand up, and rest it on the guitar in a way that feels comfortable to you. Some people like to rest their palm on the strings, some on the bridge or a pick-up ring.

Regardless of the posture you adopt, keep your hand loose. If you use a pick, don't over-grip. The pick should be held lightly, with enough pressure to keep it in place but not overexerting pressure. Remember that this is just a guideline, and that sometimes to play a "pinch" harmonic or really digging in on a phrase to get a real "down-home" flavor, you are going to need to tighten your grip on the pick. Do it when it serves your musical purpose.

Experiment, observe, and strive for comfortable positioning. Chronic over-exertion while holding the pick or striking the string with the fingers can lead to tendonitis issues in the forearm. It can also lead to bad tone quality and inflection limitations.

MAKE IT REAL!

The classic technique builder to coordinate both hands on guitar is through the patient practice of scales. Why scales? After you get your basic technical conception together, scales help you to refine technique through repetition. Once you get the fingerings and note locations happening on the finger-board, you can focus on controlling the elements that build good technique. Incorporate these guideline concepts into your scale practice:

- Keep the fingering hand fingers close to the strings. When playing scales, arch the fingers to execute the notes (think "broomstick"). While we all experience some "fly-away" fingers, the closer your finger is to the string, the easier it is to execute the next note faster. Consistency here leads to cleaner, faster chops.

- Play the scales slowly, concentrating on musicality, consistency, and accuracy. Speed up the tempo as you gain more control.

- Play lightly, and don't overexert by pressing too hard. Keep your "touch" light.

- Keep your wrist fairly straight (except when playing in the low register and "stretchy" chords).

- Limit your scale sessions to 25 minutes, then take a break. Be careful with any practice material utilizing multiple repetitions for extended periods of time.

- Use a mirror to observe yourself playing.

- As far as the "picking" hand goes, consistency and lightness of "touch" are again the essential keys here. If you use a pick, experiment with playing scales first in alternate picking (down/up). Also try all downstrokes, all upstrokes, and all reverse alternate picking (up/down), but with the emphasis on alternate technique. Some players also utilize "consecutive" picking technique, where each new string gets a downstroke while ascending up the strings, or consecutive upstrokes on each new string while going high to low. This is also known as "economy picking." Guitarists playing fingerstyle can adapt the "classic" rest stroke and free stroke.

- Don't squeeze the pick too hard or stroke the string too hard (pick or fingers). Concentrate on playing lightly with a consistently uniform "attack."

- Most of these same concepts are utilized in arpeggio playing too. We'll explore these "broken chords" after we look at some harmony basics.

The beauty of incorporating scales into building technique is that after memorizing the fingerings, you can focus on the tone quality and ergonomics of executing the scale and coordinating the two hands. You'll get to the point where you don't have to constantly watch your fingering hand for note locations. This allows you to focus on observing for *issues* visually and lets your ear guide your "touch" (both hands) for tone quality. Your technique will improve through *doing* and morph into a more efficient physical and *musical* concept.

Consistent repetition is the key to successful scale practice, so don't expect improvement without practice. Just heed the time limits cited earlier. Technique learned through scale practice will be incorporated into executing *any* scalar passage encountered in improvising, playing pieces, etc., so it really pays dividends later to get this stuff together now. We'll get into more benefits of scale practice in the next chapter.

CHAPTER 2

Scales and Modes: A Mini Thesaurus of Common Scale Usage

The word "scale" is derived from the Latin/Italian word *scala*, which means "stair." Eric Blom, in his book, *Everyman's Dictionary of Music*, defines a scale as "a succession of adjoining notes, whether proceeding in ascent or descent." Vincent Persichetti in his book, *Twentieth Century Harmony*, expands the definition to include modes: "A central tone to which other tones are related can establish tonality, and the manner in which these other tones are placed around the central tone produces modality." Scales and modes have been primary building blocks in all types of music across the globe for centuries. They are the cornerstone from which we invent melody, counterpoint, and harmony. As contemporary musicians, having a thorough knowledge of scales and their derivative modes is essential to our study of music. Since the study of scales is so big and multifaceted, I'm limiting this chapter to cataloging some of the more commonly used varieties and their derivative modes as applied to the guitar.

There are many scales out there to study. If you really want to go crazy, check out Nicholas Slonimsky's *Thesaurus of Scales*. This is *the* definitive work on scales and a great reference source. Scales are constructed of whole and half steps, with the occasional "giant step" or minor third interval showing up. (See the "*Harmony Primer*" in chapter 3 for more information about building scales.) They can be constructed of varying amounts of notes. Common scales in the jazz player's palette are pentatonic scales (constructed of five notes), blues and whole-tone scales (containing six notes), seven-tone scales (which make up the bulk of Western music's scalar vocabulary, such as the major scale, harmonic minor, etc.), octatonic or symmetrical-diminished scale (eight notes), chromatic scale (all twelve notes), and varying amounts of notes in "artificial" or "composite" scales.

MAJOR SCALE FINGERINGS

Before I list some of these scales, let's think about fingering orientation on the guitar by starting with the most common of all the Western scales, the major scale.

Fig. 2.1. C Major Scale

The major scale can be navigated in many ways on the fingerboard. If you think in terms of moving in different directions—north, south, east, and west (or up, down, and side to side), along with diagonals—you can find many possible note locations for your scales. And that doesn't even account for the fingerings! Your perspective of the directions can be from behind the guitar neck, or looking at the high strings as being "north" vs. "south," etc. Whatever helps!

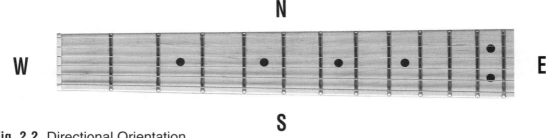

Fig. 2.2. Directional Orientation

Major scales can be played in one, two, and three octaves (in most cases) on the guitar. Most of the examples to follow are in two-octave form (approximately). Major scales are a great place to start with because their fingering shapes can be altered to produce other seven-tone scales and their variants (common modes), as well as many non-seven-tone scales that fit within the fingering shapes.

In-Position Fingerings

There are many ways of fingering scales. The "classic" Berklee way was through the *position* concept. Joe Pass and Howard Roberts also taught similar systems. Position playing was primarily organized as a tool to organize blocks of tonal (major or minor) musical activity within a limited range of frets. It was also a convenient way to teach sight-reading. Roughly speaking, in a position, each finger corresponds to a fret, with the first and fourth fingers sometimes stretching an additional fret (first finger to the left or west, and the pinky to the right or east, or vice versa if you're playing lefty). The idea here was to train the hand to play in a "box" of activity so one could improvise or read music without having to look at the fingerboard while playing. Many of us started out with this concept, and there's a lot of value in organizing some of our fingerings this way.

Here are some "in position" fingerings for the major scale. All examples are in the key of C; circled numbers are strings, and plain digits are fingers counting from the index finger as "1." Notice that many of these fingerings exceed the range of the scale's tonic and incorporate as many diatonic notes from the scale as will fit in a position. This will help to locate and finger modes related to parent major scales. More later!

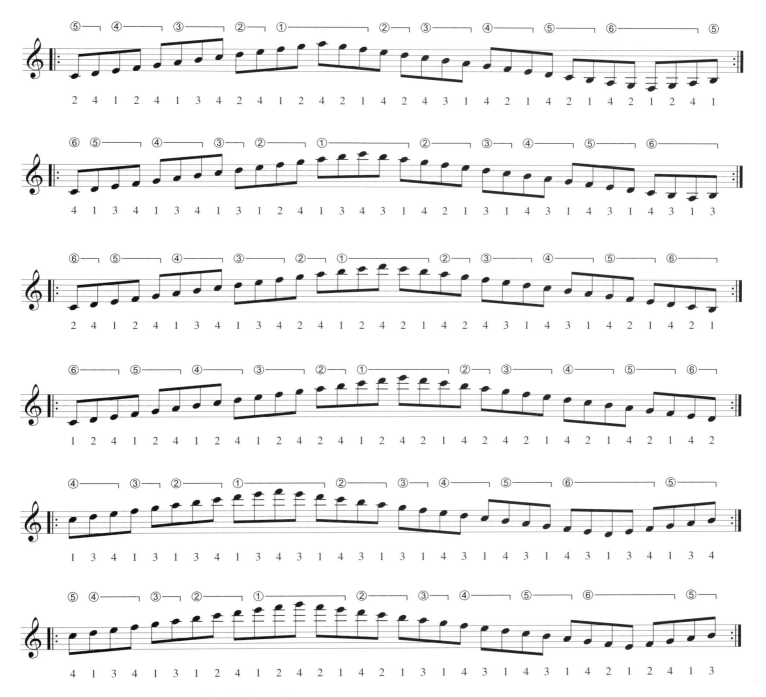

Fig. 2.3. Six In-Position Major Scale Fingerings

Keep in mind that these "master" major scale fingerings can be changed to any other seven-tone scale form by altering the basic 1 2 3 4 5 6 7 formula and changing the fingering accordingly. For instance, the formula for a harmonic minor scale is: 1 2 ♭3 4 5 ♭6 7 1. Take any of the previous major scale fingerings, lower the third and sixth degrees by a half step (by playing those notes one fret lower), and you now have the sound of and fingering for a harmonic-minor scale.

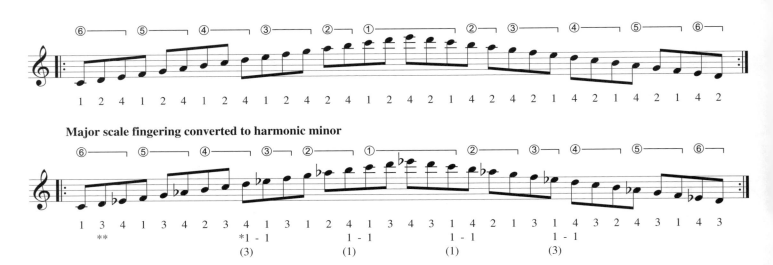

Fig. 2.4. Two-Octave C Major Scale and Conversion to C Harmonic-Minor Scale

Feel free to experiment with the fingerings. For instance, many guitarists like to slide the first finger on some of the half steps on the above harmonic minor fingering.* I've also changed a couple of fingerings—for instance, the second note D**—to give the scale a more minor-chord shape orientation. (Play a minor triad barre chord on fret 8, and you'll understand.) In-position scale fingerings are a little "stiff" but contain many arpeggio and chord shapes that are useful for improvisation and rendering musical ideas in general.

Diagonal Fingerings

Now, let's move on to some non-position fingerings.

When guitarists such as Wes Montgomery started exploring the "horn phrase," by intuitively moving over greater lengths of the fingerboard, the position concept of fingering started coming up short, especially when it came to phrasing jazz sounds in a modern way. Jim Hall also had some very unique fingering concepts himself, and Wes along with Jim heavily influenced the next great generation of jazz guitarists in their phrasing/location concepts.

One way to start moving in this direction is to play scales and their deriva-tive modes more "diagonally." Here are two major scale forms that we can use as "master" diagonal fingerings. Both fingerings extend beyond two octaves. This keeps the pattern continuing to another string, which helps facilitate real-izing other modes.

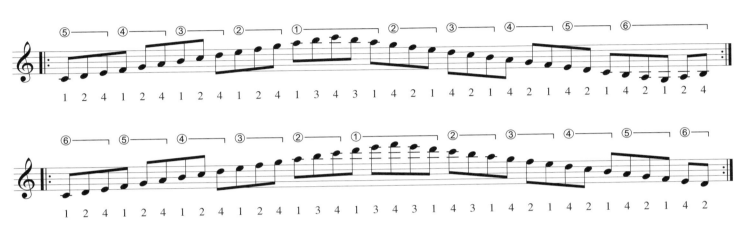

Fig. 2.5. Two-Octave Three-per-String C Major Scale Fingerings

This kind of fingering became widespread in the '70s and '80s. Commonly known as "three per string," this organizational concept helped open the door to guitarists learning not only the primary seven-tone scales, but their modes as well. So, time to take a look at modes!

Modes are notes of a scale that are reordered. An easy way to look at constructing modes comes from these three-per-string fingerings. You'll notice that the two "diagonal" fingerings for the major scale start with the first finger. Let's start with the diagonal fingering for the C major scale on the fifth string. Play the major scale, then staying on the fifth string, go to the next note in the C scale, which is D. Play the notes that are diatonic to C major (c d e f g a b c), but starting from the note D with your first finger. Play from D to D two octaves. The result is a D Dorian mode. This method of creating modes is known as *derivative*. Continue to "derive" modes by moving up the scale degrees of C major starting on the same string, with the first finger starting each new mode and playing three notes per string through the alphabetic sequence of each mode. Of course, these scales/modes can be executed in position, as well. Here are the C major scale (also known as Ionian mode) and its derivative modes in one-octave form.

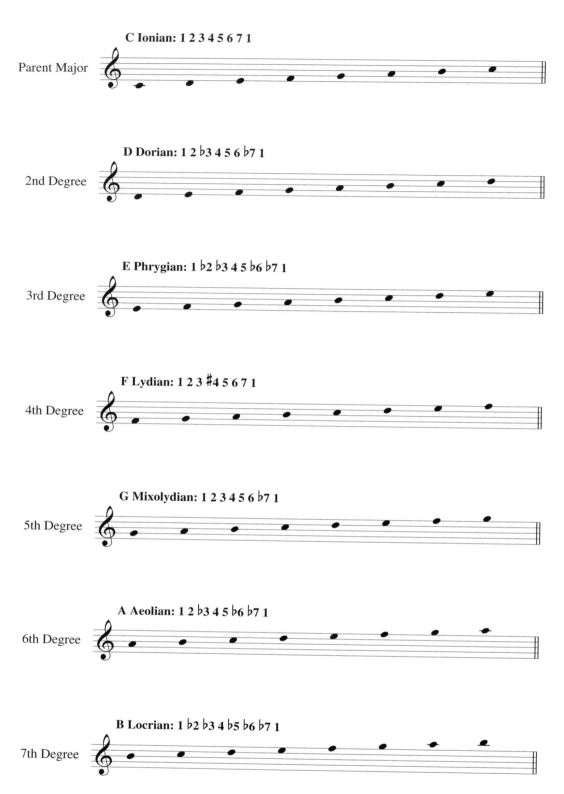

Fig. 2.6. C Ionian and Derivative Modes

Once again, as you can see, the modes of the C major scale are just a reordering of the same pitches starting from the different scale degrees. With the three-per-string concept, you move up the neck through the modes with each new scale (mode), starting with finger 1. Each new string of three notes begins with the first finger.

Here are a couple of examples in two-octave form.

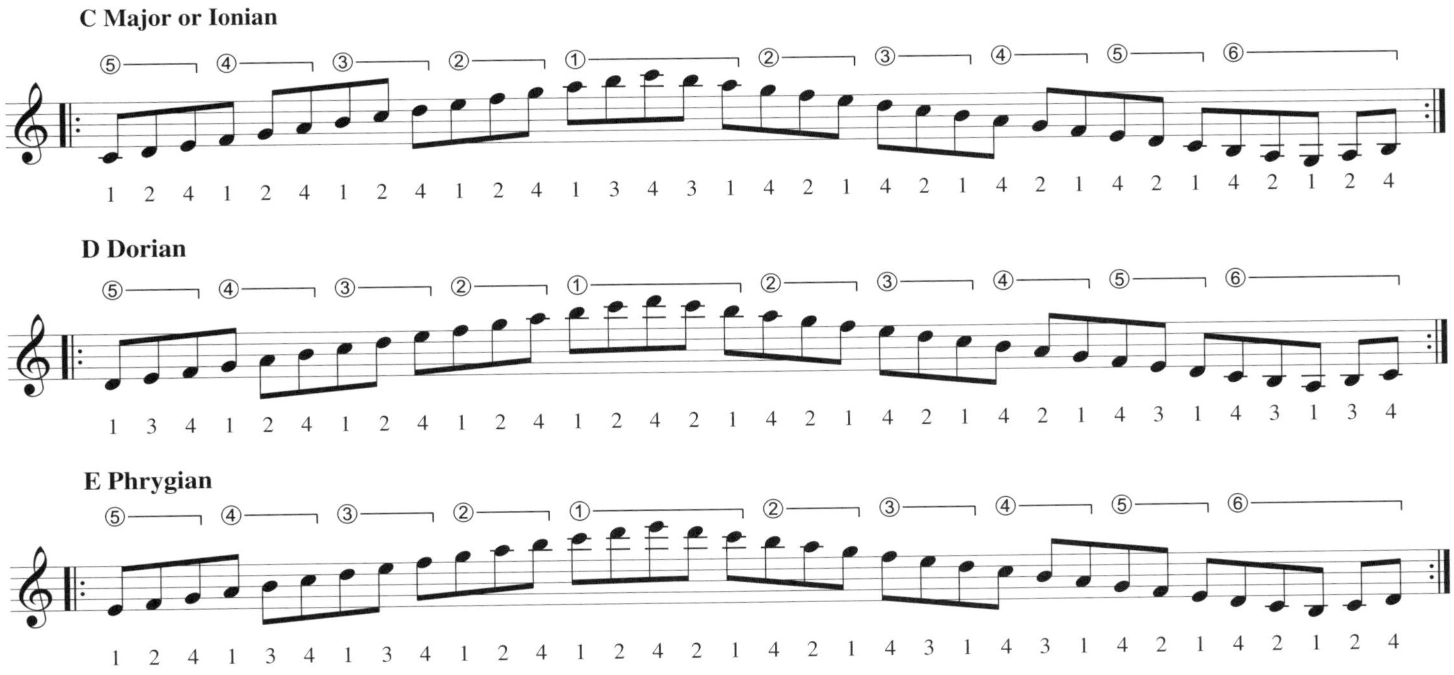

C Major or Ionian

D Dorian

E Phrygian

Fig. 2.7. Two Octave Three-per-String Fingerings for C Major, D Dorian, and E Phrygian

Feel free to put these scale shapes into pictographic form, and start transposing the scale fingerings to other tonics. Then try the parent major and derivative modes from the sixth string fingering. Depending on the parent major key and fingering, some keys (like F starting on the sixth string) will fit all seven scales ascending up the same starting string (six) within a comfortable range on the neck. Other keys might start in the middle of the neck, then run out of comfortable fingerboard room and necessitate moving to the bottom of the neck, or to a starting point on another string, to comfortably continue through the modes.

You'll notice that in figure 2.6, with the derivative modes of the major/Ionian scale, there is also a numeric formula. In addition to the three per string, we can now go back to the six major-scale "in position" fingerings mentioned previously and apply the numeric formulas for the modes to each individual major-scale fingering. Each of these major-scale fingerings can be altered and refingered to yield six additional modes via what is known as "parallel construction." Figure 2.4 shows the parallel construction of a harmonic-minor scale being created from altering the notes of the major scale. You can see, then, that major scales are a great place to start with because their fingering shapes can be altered to produce other seven-tone variants.

Speaking of variants, it's time to explore the three other seven-tone scales and their modes that we use in the Berklee guitar syllabus. These scales are the melodic minor (aka jazz minor), harmonic minor, and harmonic major. Bear in mind that an alteration of the major scale and the given fingerings will yield these new scales and their offshoot modes. Melodic minor is basically the same notes as a major scale with the third degree flatted (1 2 ♭3 4 5 6 7), making it a minor scale. (More specifically, this is the *real melodic minor* scale, as opposed to *traditional melodic minor*, which flats the 7 and 6 when descending melodically; we'll use just "melodic minor" in this book.) Harmonic minor flats the third and the sixth (1 2 ♭3 4 5 ♭6 7). The harmonic-major scale flats the sixth (1 2 3 4 5 ♭6 7).

Plug these new scales and their modes into your major scale fingerings by altering the 1 2 3 4 5 6 7 formula. Think "in-position" and "diagonal" for fingerings, and parallel and derivative for construction. Here are these three scales and their modes notated in one-octave form.

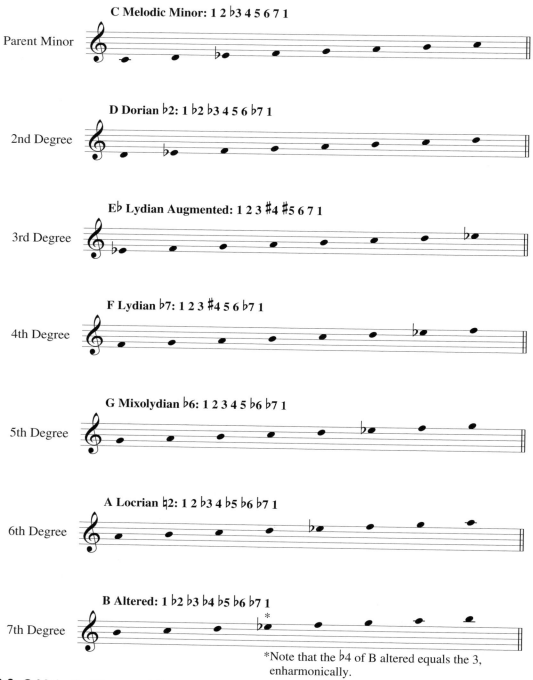

*Note that the ♭4 of B altered equals the 3, enharmonically.

Fig. 2.8. C Melodic Minor and Derivative Modes

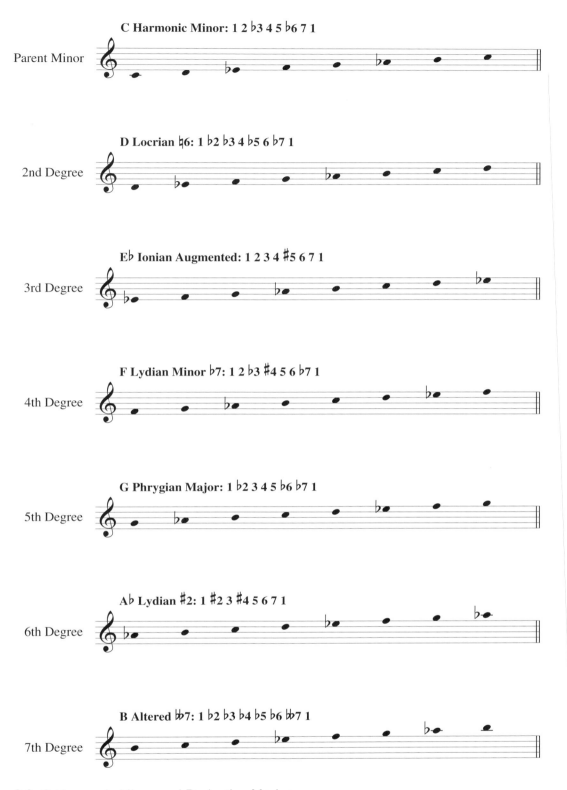

Fig. 2.9. C Harmonic Minor and Derivative Modes

NAMING MODES OF HARMONIC MINOR AND HARMONIC MAJOR

The modes of harmonic minor/major are not exactly household names. Designations like altered ♭♭7 come mainly from analysis. These scales are more commonly referred to as mode 2, mode 3, etc. of harmonic minor/major, or harmonic minor/major from the second degree, etc.

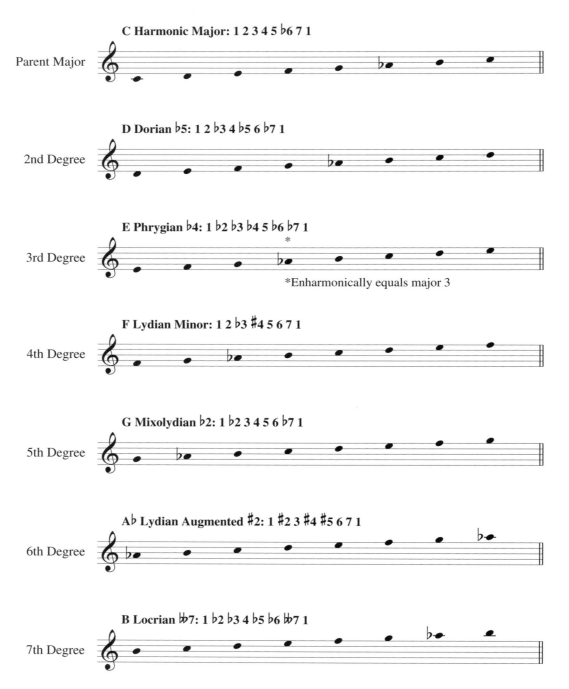

Fig. 2.10. C Harmonic Major and Derivative Modes

CHROMATIC, WHOLE-TONE, DIMINISHED, AND PENTATONIC/BLUES SCALES

In addition to the previous seven-tone scales, there are many other scales that are commonplace in compositional and improvisational usages. Five additional scales that Berklee's guitar department focuses on are the chromatic scale, the whole-tone scale, the diminished scale, the pentatonic scale, and the blues scale. These scales are very "guitar-friendly." Because of the guitar's tuning in fourths, these scales and their offshoot sequences tend to form geometric shapes and patterns on the fingerboard. These "shapes" have many constant structure aspects that make them easy to visualize, to finger, and to transpose the fingerings symmetrically. Check out some of Pat Martino's writing and videos on this subject. While the previous examples were shown in one octave, we will present these examples in two octaves.

The Chromatic Scale

The chromatic scale contains all twelve notes. It moves diagonally across the fingerboard in a very user-friendly pattern (an augmented triad) utilizing one finger per fret, with a couple of shifts. This scale can also be played positionally.

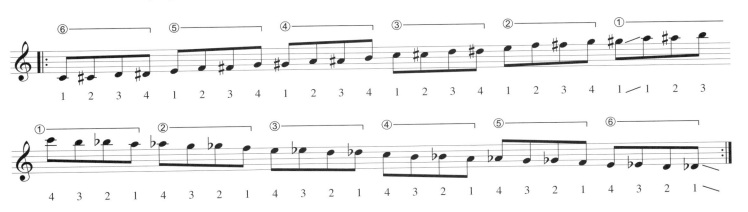

Fig. 2.11. Two-Octave Chromatic Scale

The Whole-Tone Scale

The whole-tone scale, containing six notes, has a strong connection/construction to augmented triads and augmented seventh chords, in addition to lots of other applications. There are only two whole-tone scales, as six notes divide the octave (twelve halftones) by two. The whole-tone scale can be named from any pitch within the scale you start on, but notice that the same collection of six notes and the same fingering recycle themselves every two frets, or at the interval of a major second. Notice also that the scale is comprised of two augmented triads whose roots are a second apart. The first fingering (a) is derived from one of the "in-position" major scale shapes. The second example (b) follows the shape of the augmented triad across the neck.

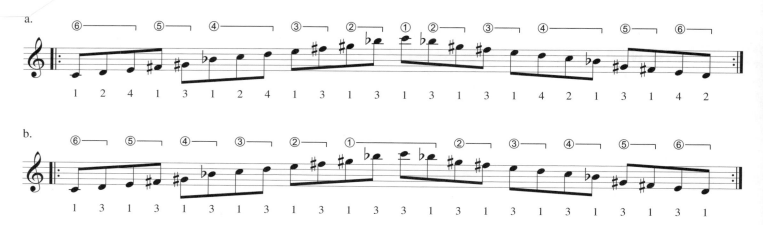

Fig. 2.12. Two-Octave C Whole-Tone Scale

The Diminished Scale

The diminished scale, also known as the octatonic scale, contains eight notes. Constructed by a formula of constant whole-step/half-step, or half-step/whole-step intervals, the scale repeats itself after eight notes using this formula. There are three diminished scales, which repeat themselves in minor thirds. The minor thirds divide the octave (twelve half steps) into four groups. Obviously related to the diminished seventh chord, the scale like the chord and its fingering repeat with the same collection of notes at the interval of a minor third. The diminished scale has strong improvisational applications over the diminished-seventh and dominant-seventh chords (dominant seventh with diminished characteristics ♭9, ♯9, ♯11, 13). This scale has been widely used compositionally in diverse contexts from composers such as Alban Berg to many great writers of film and television scores. Check out some of the old Adam West *Batman* series from the 1960s and Oliver Nelson's writing on Wes Mongomery's version of "End of a Love Affair."

Here's the whole-step/half-step version. Notice the direct connection to the C°7 chord and its symmetric inversions E♭°7, G♭°7, and A°7.

Fig. 2.13. Two-Octave Diminished Scale from C

This next version is the half-step/whole-step formula. It could also be thought of as a D♭ whole/half starting on C. (An easier way to think of this is to play a diminished whole/half formula starting from the ♭9, 3, 5, and ♭7 of a dominant 7 chord you wish to add diminished qualities to.) Notice its relationship to C7(♭9) and the other dominant chords moving symmetrically in minor thirds around it: A7(♭9), G♭7(♭9), and E♭7(♭9). Furthermore, the diminished characteristic tensions ♭9, ♯9, ♯11, and 13 can be attached to these four chords. The chord shapes will transpose, drawing tensions from the scale on each structure. For instance, C7(♭9,13), A7(♭9,13), G♭7(♭9,13), and E♭7(♭9,13) can all be spelled from the same C half/whole diminished scale, and the same chord shape (grip) moved in minor thirds produces the same structure (♭9,13) on all four roots (C, E♭, G♭, and A). The chord tones are drawn from the diminished scale, shown.

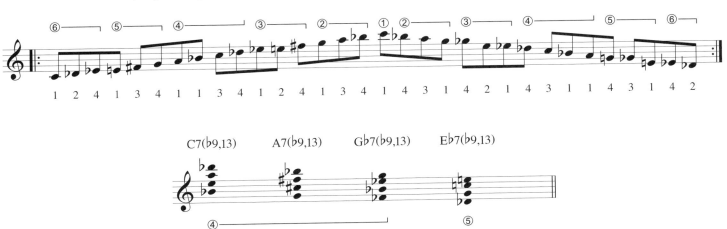

Fig. 2.14. Two-Octave Diminished Half/Whole over Dominant 7.

The Pentatonic Scale

Pentatonic scales and their usages are a big subject. The two pentatonic scales focused in the Berklee guitar syllabus are the *major six* (1, 2, 3, 5, 6) and the *minor six* (1, 2, ♭3, 5, 6). Both scales contain five notes and can be played from any note in the scale, which creates modes. The major pentatonic starting from note one has an obviously strong relationship with a major sixth chord.

Fig. 2.15. C Major Six Pentatonic

But while the major six pentatonic version has a strong major quality, we guitarists more typically use the scale from its fifth note, creating the "classic" minor seventh pentatonic.

Fig. 2.16. A Minor Seven Pentatonic

In a two-octave version, many of us learn this fingering/location first.

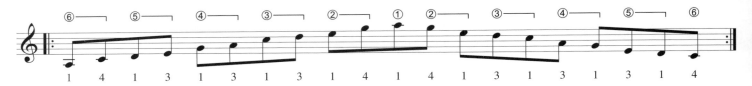

Fig. 2.17. A Minor Seven Pentatonic Two-Octave with Fingering

By lowering the third note of the major pentatonic (figure 2.15), we now have the minor sixth pentatonic (1, 2, ♭3, 5, 6).

Fig. 2.18. C Minor Six (2) Pentatonic Two-Octave with Fingering

There are many ways to finger these scales. Try the major and minor sixth pentatonics fingered (left hand) 124, 13 (1, 2, 3, 5, 6 in major), and 134, 13 (1, 2, ♭3, 5, 6 in minor) on sets of two strings like the three-octave version that follows later in this chapter. Naming these pentatonic scales and their modes is not like the seven-tone scales and their offshoots. There are no familiar scale names like Dorian, or name tags other than the analysis/description of the scale quality such as major or minor, and other characteristics that can be related to a chord or scale degree like degree (2) or degree (4) on a minor sixth pentatonic to help keep things straight. The A minor seven pentatonic (figure 2.17) is an example. This could also be called mode five of a C major six pentatonic.

As you can see, you can create many variations just by changing a note or two or inverting the scale order. Here are some commonly used pentatonics and their relationships to some harmonies for improvising. Try changing the notes of the previous major and minor scales' fingerings to locate these new scales on the fingerboard. Also experiment with more diagonal fingerings. Look ahead to the pentatonic three-octave fingerings and try the 3/2 scheme in two octaves, as well as three octaves.

This is the previously shown minor seven pentatonic, but now with a ♭5. Look familiar? I've written it starting on A again. Try improvising with it over A–7♭5. Note that this is the previous scale (figure 2.18) starting on A. Also try using it over C–6, E♭Maj7(♯11), F7, and B7(alt).

Fig. 2.19. A Minor Pentatonic with ♭5

More to try:

- C Minor Six Pentatonic with 4. Try improvising with it over C−6, E♭Maj7(♯11), F7, and B7(alt).

Fig. 2.20. C Minor Six Pentatonic with 4

- C Major Pentatonic ♭6. Try improvising on this over B♭7(♯11).

Fig. 2.21. C Major Pentatonic with ♭6

- C Major Pentatonic with ♭2. Try improvising on this over C(♭9,13).

Fig. 2.22. C Major Pentatonic with ♭2

The Blues Scale

One last scale to add to our collection here: the blues scale. While containing six notes (and therefore, technically not a pentatonic scale), it's a kissin' cousin to the minor seventh scale listed previously and definitely pentatonic derived. Its formula (1, ♭3, 4, ♭5, natural 5, ♭7) fits nicely into the pentatonic's fingering shape. In figure 2.23, A is again the tonic. Countless blues, jazz, and pop melodies and solos have been "born" from this scale and especially this particular fingering on the guitar.

Fig. 2.23. Two-Octave Blues Scale on A

That completes our list of some practical and common scales for jazz guitar. There's enough here to keep anyone busy for a long time! The key point is that the locations for these scales can be derived from shapes you've already encountered. Whether a scale is five, six, seven, or any other number of notes, there's bound to be some relationship content-wise to a fingering location from a scale fingering you already know.

Speaking of location, you'll have noticed that all of the fingerings have been in two-octave form. Two octaves is a good place to start. Many music schools audition/test their students with two-octave scales, in the early semesters. There are many good technical reasons (mentioned previously) to practice scales including two-handed coordination, for gaining flexibility of the joints, intonation focus, etc., that are essential for younger players' "guitaristic" development. Two-octave fingerings are easy to memorize, and there's a lot of visual continuity between the scale forms. Play both in position and three per string, for seven-tone scales. Pentatonic, blues, whole-tone, diminished, and chromatic scales can be in position and diagonally oriented.

THREE-OCTAVE SCALES

In the later semesters at Berklee, students begin working in three-octave configurations of the scales previously presented. Andrés Segovia's classic book, *Major and Minor Diatonic Scales* (Columbia Music Publishing), also presents his scale fingerings in three-octave form. The easiest way to create fingerings for any three-octave scale forms is to overlap portions of the two-octave versions. You can use a fragment from a scale and then shift into another scale shape, continuing this way until you've got the three-octave form. Here are a couple of examples.

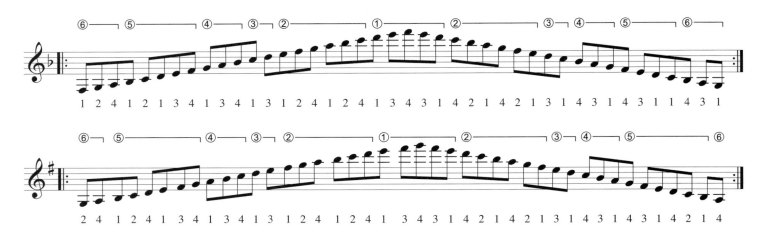

Fig. 2.24. Three-Octave F and G Major Scales

Try starting from other degrees of the scale to play related modes in three octaves, too.

Can you see the major scale forms that underlie these fingerings, in figure 2.24? Feel free to shift where you like, and convert these scales into melodic minor, harmonic minor, etc. Most seven-tone scales will derive easily from these fingerings, but chromatic, whole-tone, and diminished scales have a more "mathematical" fingering shape. One quick way (but certainly not the only way) to get fingerings for these three scales is to finger orient by the interval of a tritone (three whole steps).

FINGER ORIENTING BY A TRITONE

The three-octave chromatic scale can be played by orienting to the interval of a tritone, then filling in the chromatic notes in between. Let's start on the pitch G this time. This fingering is six notes per string. Practice "orienting" to the tritone locations first.

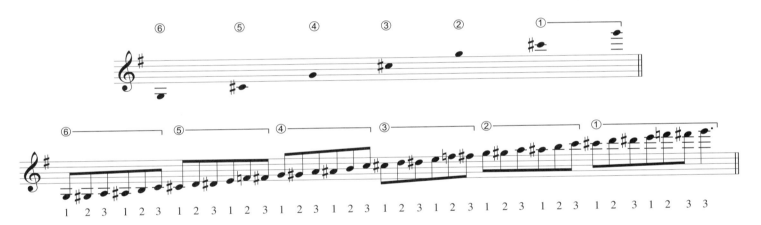

Fig. 2.25. Three-Octave Chromatic Scale Starting on G

To descend, aim for the tritone and reverse, six notes per string: ① 321, 321, ② 321, 321, etc. (There's always a double shift to complete the scale in either direction.)

The whole-tone scale in three octaves can be oriented in a similar way. Aim for the tritones, and play three notes per string, with a shift at the end in either direction.

Fig. 2.26. Three-Octave Whole-Tone Scale

The diminished scale can also be oriented toward the tritone target(s) we've been using. Ascending chromatically by string, approach the notes of the tritone from a half step below in groups of four. Descending, play directly from the notes of the tritone in groups of four notes, with a shift at the end.

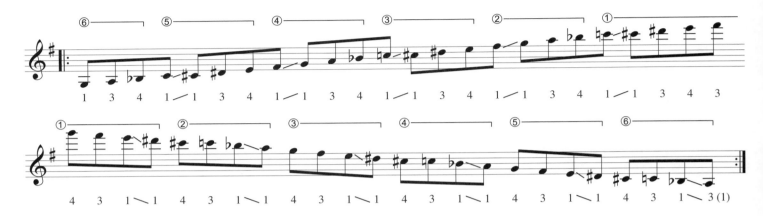

Fig. 2.27. Three-Octave G Diminished Scale

Instead of a tritone, the pentatonic scales "orient" to the interval of a fifth. The major and minor pentatonic with sixth scales fit well in a scheme of three notes on one string, two on the next, a fifth higher.

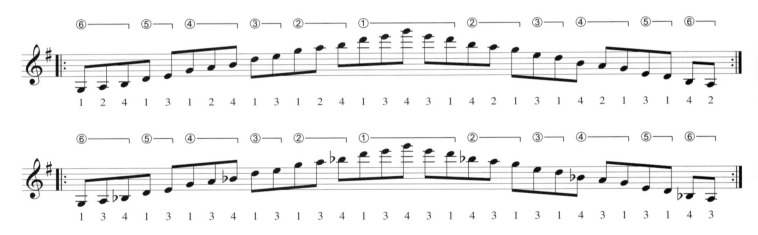

Fig. 2.28. Three-Octave G Major Six and G Minor Sixth Pentatonic Scales

These three-octave scale examples should get you started. They don't cover every fingering possibility, or for that matter, very many starting notes. Try taking similar "visual" ideas and start some fingerings on the fifth string as well. It will be necessary to play these scales in twelve keys, though in a few situations, it will be impossible to play a full three octaves on most guitars (like the key of E♭). Three-octave scale forms give us the maximum amount of register on the guitar and are a challenge to play smoothly. They also pave the way for more extreme register content in some music. Don't forget to play the scales from different degrees to play the modes from a "parent" scale.

PHRASING UP AND DOWN A STRING

There are, of course, many different ways to "realize" and phrase ideas on the guitar. Not all of them even need two or three octaves of register to execute. Many times, just a portion of a two-octave fingering moving on to another fragment of a different scale or arpeggio is the best way to move.

This last topic is what I consider to be the key ingredient of contemporary guitar playing: phrasing up and down the string length. Many of the scale examples shown here without fingerings are presented in one octave and can be played in position or diagonally. The two-octave versions can be split into halves, and there are two possible one-octave versions. But we can also begin to realize the one-octave scale versions moving up or down the neck using just one string at a time. This is a very natural thing to do on the guitar. Most of us picking up the guitar for the first time tried to pick out a melody on one string. Remember? Jim Hall in particular took advantage of organizing melodies on a single string at a time, creating a trademark sound.

Playing up a single string at a time imparts a "breathing" or horn quality to a line. This quality of phrasing became the hallmark of the next generation of great jazz guitarists. Sometimes called "the Boston School of Guitar," this concept of guitar phrasing and orientation is personified by players such as Mick Goodrick, Pat Metheny, John Scofield, Mike Stern, and John Abercrombie, among others. While this chapter is not particularly oriented towards improvisation, the use of scales plays a key role in improv content. You can begin exploring this concept by playing the preceding scales in one octave up and down a single string. A tall order, to be sure!

The benefit of two- and three-octave scales is the constant transposition and the visual aspect of a "master" scale form that can be altered by changing a note here and there to create other scales. The organizational aspect using the side-to-side concept doesn't fit into a uniform grid! First of all, each string starts with a different pitch, so the order of a scale's whole and half steps occurs in different places on each string. And you might be playing the fifth of the scale as the lowest available scale note on a string instead of orienting from the tonic. Further, because of the scale spellings in different keys, a particular scale or mode may utilize an open string, whereas another one may not. This leads to irregularities in the fingerings and a less "visual" aspect to organizing, but it's worth the effort.

Try singing the scales and melodies on one string. This is a good way to "stratify" your hearing on guitar. One string at a time becomes a manageable task, whereas the entire fingerboard and all the possibilities for movement (and learning to hear those movements) is considerably more involved!

Experiment with your fingerings, too. Connecting notes by shifting the same finger vs. using the fingers in sequence can have a very different feel and phrase quality—a very beneficial quality!

To end this topic, let's explore some ways to vary all this scale content we've learned. Scales by themselves are great technical and organizational tools. They make up a good portion of our day-to-day musical content and can be embellished by chromaticism (bop scales), etc. But they're still just scales. So once you get some of these scales together (in whatever configuration), I suggest you vary them and move them one step closer to musical application by the use of sequence.

SCALE SEQUENCES

A *scalar sequence* is a succession of notes drawn from a scale, as opposed to, say, an arpeggio or rhythmic sequence. A diatonic scalar sequence means that the succession of notes is drawn only from the pitches of that scale, in that key. Diatonic sequences are a great place to start, and almost endless variation is possible.

Start first with diatonic intervals in seconds, thirds, fourths, fifths, sixths, and sevenths. It doesn't matter which scale you use, but all the pitch choices in the sequence will be drawn exclusively from that particular scale. You'll notice that in some cases, an interval such as a third will sometimes be major and sometimes minor because of the note choices being drawn only from the set of pitches contained in the scale at hand (diatonic).

This is a one-octave sequence of diatonic thirds in C major. Try it in various positions and playing up/down the fifth and fourth strings.

Fig. 2.29. C Major Scale in Diatonic Thirds

This is a one-octave sequence of diatonic fourths in C major. Try it in various positions and playing up/down the fifth and fourth strings.

Fig. 2.30. C Major Scale in Diatonic Fourths

These diatonic interval studies can be configured in one-, two-, or three-octave versions. The one-octave sequences can be fingered in position, diagonally, and side-to-side, moving up and down the neck on just two strings. The two-octave sequences can be played diagonally, in position, as well as side-to-side (you'll need two or more sets of two strings to complete the extra range). Three-octave versions can be combinations of all three fingering methods.

When you get the major scale sequences down, you might begin to explore the derivative modes in sequences. Then try using a different parent scale, such as the melodic minor, and develop sequences from its offshoot modes.

This is a one-octave sequence of diatonic thirds in C Dorian. Try it in various positions and playing up/down the fifth and fourth strings.

Fig. 2.31. C Dorian Scale in Diatonic Thirds

This is a one-octave sequence of diatonic thirds in C melodic minor. Try it in various positions and playing up/down the fifth and fourth strings.

Fig. 2.32. C Melodic Minor in Diatonic Thirds

In addition to the interval sequences, we can use any combination of scale numbers to create sequences. These "number" sequences can work in groups of three, four, five, whatever you prefer. Some major scale examples could be:

Fig. 2.33. Two C Major Scale Sequences

Sequences can be a very useful tool for learning how to hear on the guitar. Completion of a sequence coordinates the ear with the fingers in the rendering of these basic melodies. While there are countless permutations, try getting just a few together at first. Try playing them in twelve keys and explore the different possibilities for fingering in one-, two-, and three-octave configurations. All the scales presented here (major, melodic minor, harmonic minor, harmonic major, and all their modes, along with the chromatic, whole-tone, diminished, pentatonic, and blues scales) can be utilized for sequences. Keep an "ear out" for use of sequences by your favorite players, and experiment with their usage in your improvisations and compositions.

MAKE IT REAL!

Organize a timetable for learning all the scales presented. You might study one type of scale for a month. Maybe, pick a different key each day, and practice two-octave scales, then three-octave scales, and then one octave up individual strings.

You can download the Berklee Guitar Department syllabus as a guide (classes.berklee.edu/gr). Devise a realistic set of goals for yourself.

CHAPTER 3

Harmony Primer: How Musical Devices Work

Let's discuss the derivation of basic jazz harmony and how it can be applied to the guitar. Chapter 2 details a lot of scales and fingerings; this chapter explores the process of building scales and their relationship to harmony.

Scales are, of course, melodic, but scales also contain *arpeggios* (aka "broken chords"), and when tones of a scale are played simultaneously, we get intervals and harmony. Chords and scales are inseparable, hence the study of *chord/scale theory*.

Musicians of all instruments practice scales to obtain flexibility, good intonation, and touch, among other things. The *major scale* in particular is very important not only for its value as a compositional/improvisation generator and as a technical practice tool, but as a conveyor of music formulas, as well. All melodic and harmonic musical activity can be represented in numerical code derived from major scale degrees. A chord symbol, such as CMaj7, is typically described by a formula, in this case 1, 3, 5, 7. These numbers represent tones of the major scale built on the same starting note as the root of the given chord. Altering scales by using accidentals (sharps, flats, and naturals) can lower or raise a note, which in turn, relate to other scales and create other chord types.

The starting point or name of a scale is called its tonic and is numbered as 1. All major scales, regardless of key, are given the formula 1 2 3 4 5 6 7 (8/1), which represents the scale degrees.

Scale Degrees: 1 2 3 4 5 6 7 8/1

Fig. 3.1. C Major Scale

A chord is reckoned from its root. In this case, C is the root, or 1. Tones 1, 3, 5, 7 of the C major scale sounded simultaneously = CMaj7. Notes 1, 3, 5, 7 played staggered are called arpeggios (broken chords).

Fig. 3.2. CMaj7 Arpeggio and Chord

The major scale may be altered to produce new scales, which in turn create new harmonies. For example, this scale is called Mixolydian and contains the chord C7 (1, 3, 5, ♭7) when oriented from note 1.

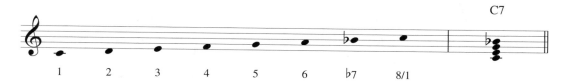

Fig. 3.3. C Mixolydian Scale and C7 Chord

To gain control of this material, you need to be able to construct scales and/or chords from any pitch, altering the major scale's formula to create other scales and chords. Let's take a closer look at the construction of a major scale.

A major scale is a seven-tone scale. It moves sequentially from its starting point, called the scale's tonic, through the musical alphabet letters ABCDEFGA, FGABCDEF, CDEFGABC, etc. Music students often learn the sound of this scale through the solfege syllables Do, Re, Mi, Fa, Sol, La, Ti, Do.

The recognizable quality of this scale comes from its arrangement of half and whole steps (also called whole and half "tones"). To review, a *step* is the measurement from one scale degree to the next (a type of interval). One whole step equals two half steps. On the guitar, a half step is one fret away, like C to C♯ or F to F♯. A whole step is two frets away, like C to D or F to G.

Chromatic alterations of notes are a half step away from the note they modify. We use accidentals—sharps, flats, and naturals—to name notes, along with the alphabetic letters.

All of the alphabet letters are a whole step apart from each other except the "natural" half steps E to F and B to C, which are on adjacent frets. The total of the seven alphabet letters and the five chromatic notes (and their enharmonic equivalents, described below) between them equals twelve tones, which are Western music's building blocks. Here are the twelve notes (most common spellings), which are thus the pitches most commonly used to start major scales. Scales built on the pitches spelled as A♯, G♯, and D♯ are less commonly used than their enharmonic equivalents B♭, A♭, and E♭.

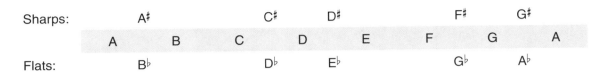

Fig. 3.4. Common Scale Starting Pitches

The notes in between the alphabet letters (chromatics) can be spelled as flats or sharps. Multiple names for the same note, for example G♭ and F♯, are known as "enharmonic equivalents." In some cases, the ("natural" half steps) B C and E F are also spelled enharmonically, like this: C♭ = B or F♭ = E.

Learning these concepts allows you to organize whole and half steps and build major scales on any pitch utilizing the step process. The formula of whole and half steps for a major scale is:

Fig. 3.5. Whole and Half Steps Forming an A Major Scale

Notice that the construction follows the alphabet sequence. You're always moving up (or down) the alphabet letters, in order, when building a seven-tone scale. There's never a question of the next note being a sharp or flat, should you need an accidental to maintain the formula, because the next note has to move alphabetically. You'll also begin to see your scales take shape with all sharps or all flats when you need to add accidentals to notes, maintaining the arrangement of whole and half steps. You've probably heard the expression "sharp keys," or "flat keys"—a very interesting organizational phenomenon that will prove extremely useful to us.

Just in case some of the above is still a little unclear (and take heart, these concepts are pretty abstract in the beginning), I've included some examples of major scales for you to look over. Analyze them in terms of the whole-step (W), half-step (1/2) formula.

Fig. 3.6. G Major Scale

Fig. 3.7. A♭ Major Scale

Fig. 3.8. B♭ Major Scale

As you get more of the major scales together, you'll notice that you're working with seven sharp scales (G, D, A, E, B, F♯, C♯) and seven flat scales (F, B♭, E♭, A♭, D♭, G♭, C♭), along with C major, which has no accidentals, for a grand total of fifteen major scales. Remember that our Western musical system only has twelve tones. These fifteen scales represent the twelve basic notes and three overlapping enharmonic equivalents. Theoretically and enharmonically, from time to time, you may need to construct a major scale on a pitch such as B♯ or the like, but the majority of your work will be with these primary fifteen major scales. These keep the use of accidentals simple, which in turn makes the reading simpler. These fifteen scales are the norm.

We've been building major scales. The word "major" also implies *tonality*—basically major or minor. A simple definition for tonality is "melodic or harmonic activity based on scales." Generally, we're working with major or minor tonality, though it is possible to be more specific, naming the scale type, for example, "Phrygian," implying certain musical attributes contained in the scales and their offshoot harmonies.

The point is that the scales we've been discussing are also tonal centers known as keys, and key is synonymous with tonality.

The *circle of fifths* is a way of ordering the common written keys, as well as listing the major scales and therefore of the major tonalities represented by these scales and keys.

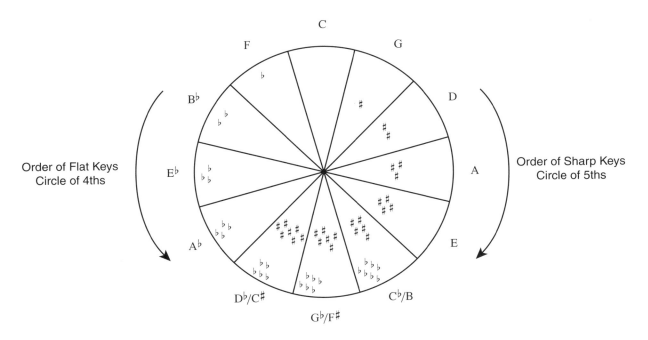

Fig. 3.9. Circle of Fifths

You'll notice that if you've written all twelve major scales that the "clock hour positions" on the circle correspond to the number of accidentals (1, 2, 3, etc.) in the sharp keys, or backwards for the flat keys, from 11:00 o'clock, that you'll need to add to the alphabetical scale sequence to keep the formula of whole and half steps intact.

Sharp Keys - clockwise	**Flat Keys** - counterclockwise (think of 11:00 as being a reverse 1:00)
Key of G 1 sharp at 1:00	Key of F 1 flat at 11:00
Key of D 2 sharps at 2:00	Key of B♭ 2 flats at 10:00
Key of A 3 sharps at 3:00	Key of E♭ 3 flats at 9:00
Key of E 4 sharps at 4:00	Key of A♭ 4 flats at 8:00
Key of B 5 sharps at 5:00	Key of D♭ 5 flats at 7:00
Key of F♯ 6 sharps at 6:00	Key of G♭ 6 flats at 6:00
Key of C♯ 7 sharps at 7:00	Key of C♭ 7 flats at 5:00

This brings us to the subject of key signatures. Key signatures are a shortcut method to building scales (and therefore, revealing what notes can be used in building chord structures—or anything else that can be represented by a numerical formula). The order of sharps and flats in key signatures can be memorized via a word phrase. The sharp keys:

Fig. 3.10. Sharp Keyword Phrase

To build a major scale from one of the sharp keys, pick the name of the scale (key), then think of the alphabet letter immediately preceding the key (or scale) name. For instance, if you're building an A major scale, think down to G, and include all the sharps from the beginning of the word phrase until you get to G (Fat Cat Guitarists). The key of A has three sharps: F, C, and G. If you plug these three sharps into the alphabetical sequence of notes written A–A, you will have the proper arrangement of whole and half steps. (See figure 3.5.)

Fig. 3.11. Sharp Key Signatures

To build a major scale from one of the flat keys, think the scale (key) name, say the flats keyword phrase up to that letter, and add one more flat. For instance, the key of B♭ has two flats, B♭ and E♭. The only exception to this method is the key of F. It has only one flat: B♭.

Fig. 3.12. Flat Keyword Phrase

Fig. 3.13. Flat Key Signatures

You can now construct (with a little practice) major scales in fifteen keys. Don't forget that the key of C is neutral and has no accidentals at all. You can write them using the whole-step, half-step method, or you can plug the key signatures into the blank alphabet sequences to get the correct step order. Either way, you'll begin to memorize the contents of the scales and to associate the key signatures with particular keys/scales. Many times on the gig, when musicians call a tune, they *might* also give you the key by saying "three flats" (key of E♭), or "one sharp" (key of G).

CHORDS AND VOICINGS

We can construct scales and harmonies in any key or on any root by interpreting a formula relative to a major scale. So, without further ado, here are the harmonic formulas for the four triadic types and the eleven primary seventh chords. All numbers and chromatic alterations relate to a major scale starting on the same note as the chord's root. In this case, the scale is C major.

Fig. 3.14. Triads

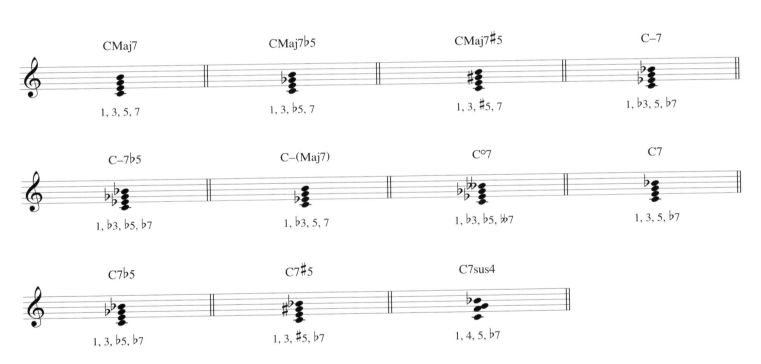

Fig. 3.15. Seventh Chords

There are a few other common harmonic structures you might notice missing from above. Major sixth and minor sixth chords will become part of the major and minor seventh chords in terms of *tensions* (we'll go over these soon). Another structure, sometimes labeled as minor7♯5, also will be covered later.

By applying these harmonic formulas relative to the major scales you have been creating, you will be able to construct all triads and seventh chords from any root. The problem is, playing these chords on the guitar from the stacked thirds (particularly seventh chords) can be difficult, if not just impossible! We need to make these chords "guitar friendly," so let me introduce you to different ways of creating guitar chord *voicings*, or vertical note arrangements.

POSITIONS (INVERSIONS)

The number of tones in a chord determines how many positions (or "inversions") a chord can be arranged in. Triads, having three notes, have three positions: *root position*, where the root is the lowest note in the chord; *first inversion*, where the third is the lowest note; and *second inversion*, where the fifth is the lowest note. These chords can be placed in any octave, higher or lower. The position's name is determined by the lowest note.

These chords can be placed in any octave higher or lower and the naming of the position will still be determined by the lowest note.

Fig. 3.16. Triadic Inversions

CLOSE VS. SPREAD VOICINGS

The word "position" also conveys another descriptive term relative to the spacing of the chord tones. There are two classifications: *close position* (sometimes called "tight"), where, in all inversions, each note is as close as possible to the next (above or below), and *open position* (sometimes called "spread," in the case of triads), where the chord tones are more spread out—more than an octave. In triadic chords, most modern jazz guitarists refer to open-position triads as "spread triads."

Close position voicings

To open (spread) a close position triad, simply move the middle note (or voice) of the chord up or down an octave.

Spread - Middle note up an octave

Spread - Middle note down an octave

Fig. 3.17. Close and Spread C Major Triads in All Positions

Notice that whether you move the middle voice up or down, you get the same three voicings. There's just a difference in octaves. Try moving through the positions of the triads and convert to all types: major, minor, diminished, and augmented in both close and spread formats. These voicings can be played across, up, and in combinations (diagonally) over the fingerboard.

You'll notice that the term "voice" is now being used in place of "note." Each note in a chord is known as a voice. Terms like voicing and voice leading refer to how we construct and connect harmony.

Now that you have encountered triads, let's look at the seventh chords in terms of positions and voicing. A seventh chord has four tones and therefore four positions (once again, regardless of octave register). We'll use C7 as an example, but the method is the same for all types of seventh chords.

Fig. 3.18. Close Position C7 Chords

DROP VOICINGS

If you try to play these voicings on guitar, you'll find them difficult or impossible to play without changing octaves. Even then, they sound pretty "thin" as well as being really difficult to "grab" quickly. *Drop voicings* is the way to make them usable!

Drop voicings are easy to make and create very standard chord forms for the guitar. They sound richer than their close-position cousins. They're much easier to play physically and "lie" better on the guitar fingerboard. In addition to their usefulness for guitarists, they are widely used by all chord instrumentalists (vibraphonists, pianists, etc.) and arrangers.

To construct drop voicings from close position:

1. Each tone in the four-part chord is called a voice.

2. The voices are numbered voice 1, voice 2, voice 3, and voice 4. The highest note is assigned voice 1. The lowest is voice 4.

3. Drop a designated voice (such as 2 or 3) an octave, while leaving the other voices where they were.

The most commonly used drop-voicings formulas are: drop 2, drop 3, and drop 2&4. Let's start with the drop-2 voicing. Much of traditional jazz harmony vocabulary on guitar comes from these structures.

C7 Close Position   **C7 Converted to Open Position Drop-2**

Fig. 3.19. C7 Close and Drop-2

You can change the octave and the chord spelling remains the same.

Fig. 3.20. C7 Drop-2 Voicings Up an Octave

A drop-2 voicing (voice 2 drops an octave) always encompasses four adjacent strings on the guitar. We could play the lower version of the chords with the bottom notes moving up the sixth string and then transfer the bottom notes on the fifth string and finally the bottom notes on the fourth string as the chords get higher.

You could play all four positions of the C7 on a single string set: 6543, ♯5432, ♯4321.

Fig. 3.21. Drop-2 Voicings Moving Up and Across String Sets

Drop-3 voicings (voice 3 drops an octave) encompass five strings and can also be organized by string groups (6x5432 and 5x4321). There's always a muted string in drop-3 voicings; the "x" in the string group indicates a muted string.

Fig. 3.22. C7 Drop-3 Voicings Moving Up Two String Groups

Drop 2&4s can be done with the same method, though they're not as widely used as the drop-2 and drop-3 voicings. Check them out, too! One thing I'll warn you about with all these chords: Some chord types are possible to play pretty easily, and others might be physically difficult or nearly impossible for you to play.

MAKE IT REAL!

Go through the possibilities in all keys with all eleven chord types. Make a note of the chord voicings you like sonically and for ease of fingering, and start using them in tunes. This is crucial for developing your harmonic vocabulary.

After a discussion on fingerboard logistics in the next chapter, we begin to add tensions to these drop voicings in chapter 5. This allows us to form the "spicier" jazz chords we all crave!

CHAPTER 4

Fingerboard Logistics

MAPPING OUT THE FINGERBOARD

There are countless ways to map out fingerings and play an idea on the guitar fingerboard. Many great players have developed their unique sound, phrasing, and technique through their personal concept of mapping out musical ideas on the fingerboard. In addition to location, fingering concepts also play a key role in the musical results. In this chapter, we'll work through some concepts to help you approach navigating the guitar fingerboard.

To begin with, there are a wide range of guitarist techniques out there! Some of them use the pinky on the fingering hand, and some don't. There are a lot of killer guitarists who use just three fingers on the fingering hand when they play solo lines. There are also many great "schooled" players who use the pinky, as well. What's the issue? The phrase quality of the music and visualization of structures on the fingerboard!

A combination of both works for me. "Schooled" players usually start with scale practice, which always includes the use of the pinky on the fingering hand. As you'll have noticed in the scales chapter, all of the scale fingerings make use of the pinky.

The classic approach to two-octave scale fingerings, along with all the arpeggios and chord shapes contained within, uses the "position" method of location/fingering. Roughly speaking, a fingerboard position encompasses four frets: one for each finger. This allows you to stretch to the left with the first finger and/or stretch to the right with the fourth finger. This technique has served hordes of guitarists as a way to locate and organize fingerings, render musical ideas, and relate reading examples to keys based on scales.

But positional thinking has its shortcomings. Modern guitar technique and phrasing need to move more laterally (side-to-side) to execute the "horn phrase" and content of contemporary improv ideas. Many times, I've seen a student try to play a transcription in position because of the key orientation—yikes! Stretching fingers to the left and right while playing in a block of frets doesn't usually do justice to the musical content, phrasing, or technique. You have got to move on the fingerboard and play outside of "the box." But there is great usefulness in position playing, and we can still utilize this concept. Just break positional content up into smaller parcels; identify musical elements such as intervals, scale fragments, and chord outlines; and move into and connect them more laterally. I call this concept "smart boxes," and it helps us to keep from getting stuck in "big boxes." Sometimes, the fingering won't involve using all four fingers, and that *can* be a good thing. Let's look at some ideas to get this going in your playing.

Here's an intervallic study based predominantly on seconds. Play the interval shape, and move it freely with the given fingerings.

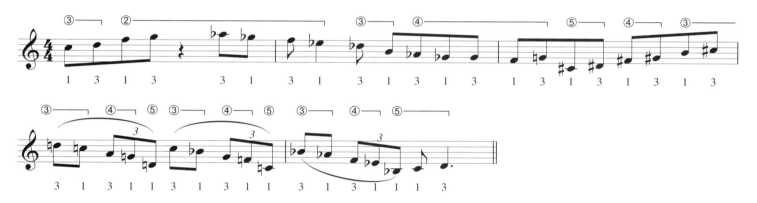

Fig. 4.1. Intervallic Study in Seconds

Here's another interval-based fingering. This time, the prevalent interval shape is a fourth. These fingerings are coming from minor seventh pentatonic-scale shapes that shift from side-to-side.

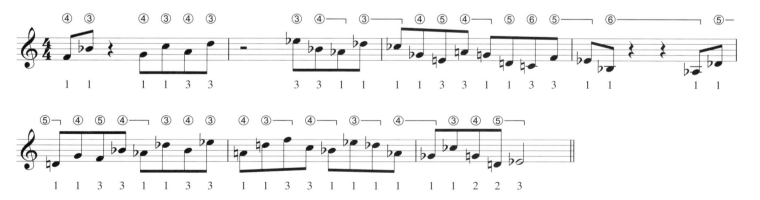

Fig. 4.2. Intervallic Study in Fourths

Play adjacent strings using the same finger with a "roll." Notice again there is no use of the fourth finger—yet. Feel free to use any fingering you like, but move the interval shapes on the designated strings.

This next example is a series of descending major triad arpeggios that resolve into an F7 chord. You could play it in position but would lose the natural and intuitive quality gained by playing it down the ②, ③, ④, ⑤ string set. Notice that each triad starts with the finger that would normally play that note within the chord shape. Only the beginning string of each triad is marked.

Fig. 4.3. Triadic Sequence

These previous three examples will get you thinking about movement on the fingerboard. Now, let's look at the smart boxes idea from a scale perspective. Anywhere there is a scale fingering, there are chord arpeggios and voicings related to that scale. Here's a C Mixolydian/F major scale exercise with a position orientation.

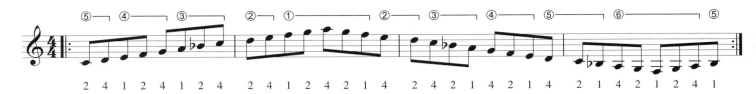

Fig. 4.4. C Mixolydian/F Major Scale Exercise

Within this big 2+ octave scale fingering lies a C7 arpeggio and C7 chord grip.

Fig. 4.5. C7 Arpeggio and C7 Chord

By using the chord outline, passing scale, and chromatic notes, we can make a jazz line.

Fig. 4.6. C7 Chord Outline

Notice this line didn't use the entire range of the previous C Mixolydian fingering. And speaking of fingering, observe that there are some unusual fingerings here. I like to group certain chromatic passages and triplets predominantly with fingers 1 to 3. I also slide the first finger from chromatics into chord tones in several spots, so there's a good bit of side-to-side motion within the scale/arpeggio/chord picture. I use the fourth finger wherever it suits the musical idea I'm trying to achieve. (You can use the fourth or third, as you like.) Like chord outlines, scalar passages can also be made of portions from a larger positional scale fingering. When you encounter chromatics or scale tones that move outside of the "box," you'll often want to favor the first finger to slide between these notes, as in this example.

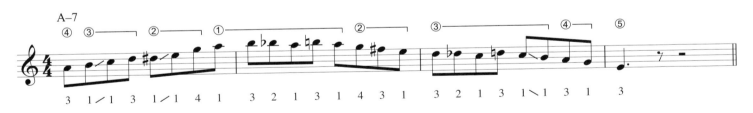

Fig. 4.7. Scale Line with Slides

But in addition to the first finger slides, scale fragments, or even entire scales, can shift into parallel patterns with any finger that makes sense.

Fig. 4.8. Major Scales Connected by Second Finger Slide

After you get the hang of the previous examples, the next move is to connect the "smart boxes," interval shapes, etc., together to execute musical ideas. Sometimes you move smoothly note-wise but jump between chord ideas from one to the next. Chord ideas can be either outlines (arpeggios) or scalar in makeup. Note that the first finger leads the move into the FMaj7 portion here. Most "jumps" like this are best played with the first finger, but there are always options. Experiment with what feels good to you!

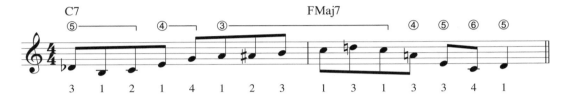

Fig. 4.9. Connecting Two Chords with a Jump

You could also try the fingering like this.

Fig. 4.10. Connecting Two Chords Alternate Fingering

Either way you choose, note that the B on beat 4+ of the first bar and C on beat 1 of bar 2 doesn't use consecutive fingers to connect. We're connecting two chord ideas together via smart boxes. The overall line fingering results from visualizing two smaller chord components. You will have noticed that we could also just play this line in position at the seventh fret, too. Go ahead, try it! You can do it, but the phrasing isn't as good as the other fingering examples and feels a little stiff.

Here's another example of jumping between chord ideas leading with the first finger.

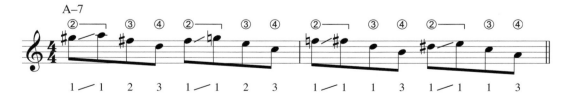

Fig. 4.11. Triadic Sequence with Jumps

Play the triad chord shapes down the same string group ②, ③, ④. These are diatonic triads (A Dorian) with a chromatic approach to the fifth of each chord. Roll the finger between adjacent strings on the same fret. Improv content-wise, this is an example of playing multiple chord ideas over a single harmony (A–7). As with the previous triadic sequence (figure 4.3), each note in the triad is played with the finger that would normally play that note within the chord shape. So, if you played figure 4.10 in reverse (low to high), you could lead each chord with the third finger.

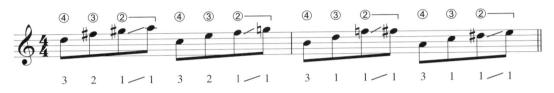

Fig. 4.12. Triadic Sequence with Jumps Led by Third Finger

Here's an example of a whole-tone scale fragment moving by jumps of a second, just to remind you that scale fragments can work this way too.

Fig. 4.13. Whole-Tone Scale Sequence

Larger sections of in-position orientation are possible, too. But, while there's a two-octave chord shape that's in position lurking underneath this line, it's the delayed chromatic resolutions along with the fingering moving laterally that makes the phrasing "happening!"

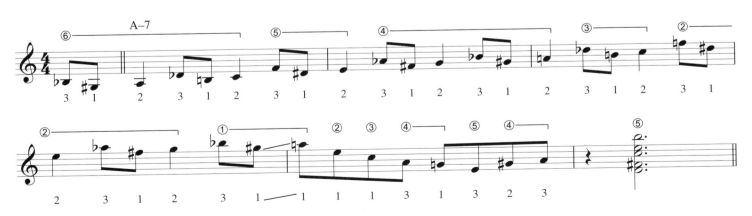

Fig. 4.14. Position Orientation with Side-to-Side Movement

That's a lot to digest! I hope you have grasped the concept of movement side-to-side while also visualizing musical components and structures. Here's an etude on the changes of a classic jazz standard ("I'm Old Fashioned"), which links many of these fingering concepts together. As far as the issue of third vs. fourth finger, sometimes I prefer the third finger over the fourth, sometimes not. It really has to do with what's coming up and where I'm coming from. This etude contains a lot of smart box usage and interval shapes that warrant the use of the third finger—and also the fourth. Try it, and see what fingering you like!

Fingering Etude

Track 1 w/Guitar
Track 2 w/o Guitar

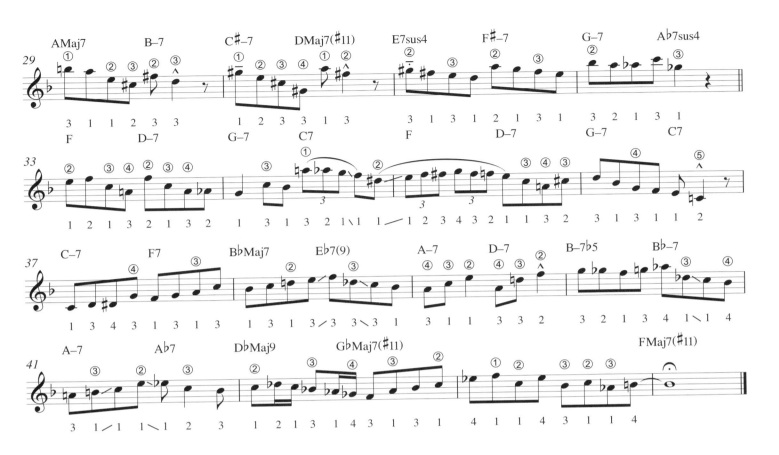

Fig. 4.15. Fingering Etude

MAKE IT REAL!

Here are some other ideas to help you map out the fingerboard:

1. Review all the ideas from chapter 2.

2. Play all scales in position, as three notes per string and on a single string at a time.

3. Try playing interval sequences both in position and moving up a pair of strings. Here's an example of diatonic thirds moving up two strings.

Fig. 4.16. C Major Scale Sequence in Thirds

Try playing seconds (on one string), fourths, fifths, sixths, and sevenths like the above example. Just change the string pairings as needed.

Investigate and learn some bop heads like Donna Lee, Half Nelson, Confirmation, and others! You'll see a lot of the same musical content as I've used in this chapter's examples. Try applying the fingering concepts presented here, and experiment with your own!

CHAPTER 5

Tensions

ADDING COLOR TONES TO BASIC CHORD STRUCTURES

Tensions, also known as "extensions" and various other terms regionally, are the color tones added to basic chords, giving them modern harmonic flavor. Tensions have an air of mystique about them. They are regarded by many younger players as complicated and time-consuming to learn. Many guitarists learn these chords by pictogram and tab, and that's okay, but I'm going to present a more in-depth method. The good news is that this information is easy to understand, and you can implement it right away. You will be able to construct any type of "advanced jazz" chord by learning this material. Of course, though the rewards are worth it, you're going to pay some dues to really get inside this material. It takes time and patience.

Let's start out by defining what a tension is: a *tension* is a tone that adds color and discord to a chord without confusing the quality (type) of the chord. This simply means that while you embellish it and make it sound more modern, etc., the chord is still recognizable as being major, dominant 7, minor 7♭5, or whatever.

Probably the best way to study the use of tensions is by period. You can study periods in jazz harmony (and use of tensions) almost by decade, and we'll be focusing our attention in this chapter on jazz harmony between 1930 and 1960. But rest assured, this material is alive and well and very much a part of present jazz harmony. It is essential language in the study of jazz guitar and an important part of all practical jazz guitarists' knowledge base.

Tensions can be applied to harmony both vertically and horizontally. This means that on a given chord structure, we can add the tensions on top of a chord or in place of one of the basic chord tones. This is vertical thinking: the chord tones and tensions sound simultaneously. Horizontal harmonic thinking about tensions is basically scale oriented. The pitches of a scale can be harmonized with notes of that scale, resulting in diatonic harmonies and tensions. These harmonized scale voicings create tension and release as one moves horizontally through the harmonized scale's harmonic structures. More commonly known as "comping by scale," this method of generating harmony was widely adopted by Bill Evans, McCoy Tyner, Chick Corea, Herbie Hancock, and many others in the late 1950s and 1960s (see chapter 6).

Our goal here is to upgrade the basic harmonies that are generated by *tertian* thinking (harmony built by thirds) as opposed to the *quartal* harmony (harmony based on fourths) so indigenous to comping by scale sounds of the 1960s. However, sometimes converting the closed harmony to open, and then adding tensions, creates intervals of fourths in a chord's makeup.

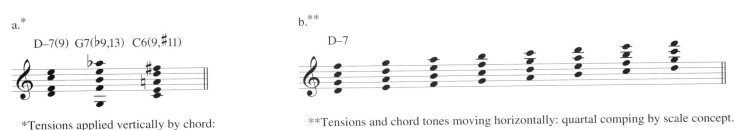

*Tensions applied vertically by chord: tertian harmony.
(Notice the fourths in the chords.)

**Tensions and chord tones moving horizontally: quartal comping by scale concept.

Fig. 5.1. Tertian and Quartal Voicings

You'll notice in figure 5.1 that the vertical-tertian chords have quite a few fourths in the chords. The addition of the tensions and the respelling of the G7(♭9,13) and C6(9,♯11) chords have resulted in some intervals of a fourth in the construction of the voicings. So, is it a fourth chord, or a tertian chord? Viewed from a construction standpoint, they have elements in common but are still tertian. In the end, tertian vs. quartal thinking is just an orientation. The final result, musically, is what counts. Sometimes musical theory produces situations that can be analyzed in more than one way, but the final judge as to its relevance is your ear. Jazz compers mix tertian and quartal voicings together freely!

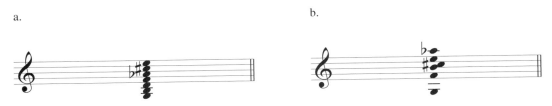

It's easy to see the thirds orientation in (a). In (b), the respelled chord still has some fourths (an augmented fourth, a perfect fourth, and a diminished fourth), even though we're "thinking" in thirds.

Fig. 5.2. (a) Thirds vs. (b) Fourths

Since we're thinking about tertian chord theory in this chapter, consider a list of tensions as they relate to the primary seventh chords that are built in thirds. A word of caution! This is a sonority-based system where the tension is used on particular chords just because it sounds good. These are "common practice" usages that are drawn mainly from the so-called "hard-bop" period (1950s). This is a different orientation from basic chord-scale theory that draws available tensions from primary diatonic scales. Some of our "sonority based" tensions violate "function intent" rules, and/or would be considered "non-diatonic" in some cases of harmonic analysis. So be forewarned; some of the tensions that we'll use here would be considered "wrong" or "unavailable" in more academic settings, at least in the more primary applications.

One additional thought: Any note can be added to any chord to achieve a desired musical effect. The listing of tensions for these particular chords is the way that Joe Pass, Wes Montgomery, Tal Farlow, and others might color a chord. But, if you wanted to go a little more in Thelonious Monk's direction, or if you were writing a score for a movie that called for some shocking sounds, you could deviate from the chart. Remember, these sounds (tensions) are a place to start from. They're in the tradition and will help you get good results musically. You need to listen to players from all periods to understand the history of usage.

Tension Chart		
Maj7: 9, #11, 13	–7: 9, 11, 13	Dom7: ♭9, ♮9, #9, #11, ♭13, ♮13
Maj7#5: 9, #11	–7♭5: 9, 11, ♭13	7#5: 9, #11
Maj7♭5: 9, ♭13	–(Maj7): 9, 11, #11, 13	7♭5: 9, ♭13
	°7: 9, 11, ♭13, ♮7	7sus4: ♭9, ♮9, ♭13, ♮13, ♭10, ♮10

Fig. 5.3. Tension Chart

The tension chart (figure 5.3) will give you good results in terms of colors that go well with the basic seventh chords. Always let your ears be the final judge. Don't be afraid to experiment!

Notice that Maj7♭5, Maj7#5, and 7sus4 are not typical bop-period chords. I've included them to round out our harmonic vocabulary. These chords really gained importance in the harmonic pallet of the 1960s and 1970s via the compositions of Wayne Shorter, Chick Corea, and others who modernized the jazz vocabulary. Also notice that Maj7#5, Maj7♭5, Dominant 7#5, and Dominant 7♭5 use rather conservative tensions on the chart. Try some of the "altered tensions" (♭9, #9, etc.), and check out the results. They may be a little too "outside" for some situations but can add some more yang to your yin! Tension and release in choosing colorization between voicings is an important factor.

By now, maybe you're trying some of these sounds out on your axe. If so, you will have noticed a big problem right away.

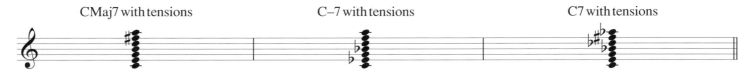

While possible for pianists, these chords are impossible to play on the guitar.

Fig. 5.4. Unplayable Chords!

Even pianists find them too big and clunky for most situations. So what do you do? Go back to chapter 3, and check out the drop voicing material. Take any of the close position seventh chords and convert them to drop-2 or drop-3 position. Here are some drop-2 voicings, for examples.

Fig. 5.5. Drop-2 Voicings

The basic seventh chord is now in a "guitar-friendly" playable position. But alas, we're still playing chords that are not very jazzy sounding. This is where we start having some fun! What we'll do is substitute tensions for low degree chord tones in the drop-voicing chords. Here's the substitution formula:

9 replaces 1

13 replaces 5

11 replaces ♭3 (on minor only)

There are other subs possible, but for now, let's keep it simple by using only these three choices. These numbers are generic. This means the quality of a 9 or 13 can be flat, natural, or sharp according to what the tension chart dictates for a particular chord type. One other condition, for the time being: Don't replace a chord tone with a tension if the chord tone is in the bottom of the voicing. This is a generalization. Use your ears, and if it sounds good, use it, but voicings using low register tension subs tend to sound ambiguous and murky. With the four positions yielded by our drop-2 voicings, and the different string groups these chords are playable on, we now have a lot of options. Unfortunately, not all the fingerings are going to be practical. Let's look at the drop-2s from the previous page and perform some integration of tensions to see what we get.

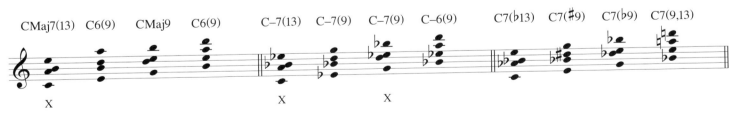

Fig. 5.6. Drop-2 Voicings with Tensions. Some would be playable using open strings.

The chords with the "X" are impossible to play without using open strings or are just too physically difficult to grab. The rest of the chords are typical "grips" and are transposable to all roots. Speaking of roots, you'll notice that many roots have been replaced with 9s. These are sometimes known as "assumed root chords," and have to be reckoned from another chord tone to transpose them properly. When most of us start learning voicings, we tend to use the root as the most visible note to transpose the closed form from one pitch to another. These "rootless chords" take a little time to get used to but are really valuable for getting "hip" sounds. Also, in a group context, those roots will be sounded or implied by the bass player, so they don't necessarily have to be doubled. All the chords contain their "guide tones" (the third and seventh, except for 7sus4 where the fourth replaces the third), which identify the chord type as major 7, minor 7, min(maj7), diminished 7, or dominant 7. The other chords with alterations to the fifth still fit into the preceding chord categories.

Tensions themselves are sometimes confusing to name due to the octave of usage. You will have noticed above that what is being listed as a thirteenth, for instance, is interval-wise often just a sixth. Some contemporary harmonic theory tends to use the lower designation when the tension is lower in the voicing, like F(2)/A as an example. Guitarists often try to get the note in anywhere they can grab it in a voicing but tend to think of a tension in terms of the higher number. The long and short of it is that 2=9, 4=11, and 6=13. The first major example (if played with open strings) in figure 5.6 could be designated as CMaj7(add 6), but it could work just fine if the chord symbol on a chart called for CMaj7(13). Sometimes theory can get too scientific, and the most important thing is to make some music. The chords in figure 5.6 are just one example of how tensions could be added to the basic drop-2 voicing. Experiment and find more variations. Try adding one tension, then maybe two, if possible.

Once you've learned the tension substitution principle, you can try writing versions of the new tension-colored chords using the basic drop-2 and drop-3 (and also drop-2&4) voicings you already know, and integrate them into your playing immediately. Writing them down is extremely helpful, at this stage. Because there are so many variations, it can become very difficult to keep track of the good voicings you come across. Eliminate the poor sounding ones or those that are too difficult to play. When you find a good voicing, you might start by transposing the shape around the fingerboard chromatically or by cycle five (or four). This will help your muscle memory retain the feel of the grip, and you'll have a better chance of executing it in performance.

Now that you know how to use tensions on basic chords, how do these chords fit into a jazz context? It is very important to listen to guitarists who utilize this vocabulary in their playing. Listen to players like Joe Pass, Wes Montgomery, Jim Hall, Pat Martino, and the other jazz guitar giants to learn, by ear (listening), their use of this vocabulary. It also helps to analyze written/transcribed examples of these kinds of harmonies. There are plenty of transcription books on the market. And very essential: the new "hip" chords you're creating progress to other chords. We need a mixture of "plain" and "spicier" voicings to get an interesting balance in comping, chord solos, etc.

Performance in different styles dictates certain ways to approach harmonic usage, too. If you're playing rhythm guitar in a Count Basie swing band style, you'll need to pare down most "big chords" with tensions to basic guide tone voicings to play in the "bag." This is an art in itself! But we're trying to emulate guys like Wes and Joe here, so where do you begin mixing tensions in your playing? Here are a couple of examples of how to start organizing your voicings. Try starting with a simple tune form, like the blues, and write whole- and half-note voicings for your progression.

On the recording are three versions of this etude: slow, fast, and fast with comping. Each variation is played twice, with a full band and a play-along track.

Voiced Blues

Track 3 - Slow w/Guitar
Track 4 - Slow w/o Guitar
Track 5 - Fast w/Guitar
Track 6 - Fast w/o Guitar
Track 7 - Comping Rhythms w/Guitar
Track 8 - Comping Rhythms w/o Guitar

Fig. 5.7. Voiced Blues

Analyze these chords, and see how the tensions have replaced low degree chord tones, discover the original drop-2 voicings lurking underneath, and learn how to finger the chords. You'll notice that I've repeated many of the same structures. Not only do they sound good, they keep the task doable.

Keep it simple. Don't bite off more than you can chew! Practice hint: When possible, find different fingerings for the same chord on different string groups.

Here's another blues, this time in F. The progression is based on Bird's tune "Blues for Alice," and the progression is more challenging. Try the same procedures we used on the last example, and start writing your own versions. Notice how I've mixed in some plain seventh chords and even a couple of three-note voicings. Yin yang, baby!

On the recording are three versions of this etude: slow, fast, and fast with comping. Each variation is played twice, with a full band and a play-along track.

Voiced Blues 2

Track 9 - Slow w/Guitar
Track 10 - Slow w/o Guitar
Track 11 - Fast w/Guitar
Track 12 - Fast w/o Guitar
Track 13 - Comping Rhythms w/Guitar
Track 14 - Comping Rhythms w/o Guitar

Fig. 5.8. Voiced Blues 2

MAKE IT REAL!

Start writing your own examples. If you're learning some bop tunes, try voicing some chords (written) on these progressions and listen to the masters working their magic on them! Emulate what you like! Check out the appendix containing gridded forms to help you find some good examples of usable voicings.

CHAPTER 6

Quartal Harmony: Comping by Scale

Quartal harmony is generated by the interval of a fourth. This concept of jazz harmony developed in the mid 1950s and the early 1960s, spurred on by the widespread use of modalism by such artists as Miles Davis and John Coltrane, and their group members. Already long in use by "classical" composers, composers of film and television scores, and jazz composers/arrangers from the Gil Evans school, quartal harmony had became an important tool in jazz vocabulary by the early 1960s. In addition to the composer/arranger usage, quartal harmonic language was ushered into jazz largely by the comping, improvising, and compositions of pianists Bill Evans, McCoy Tyner, Herbie Hancock, and Chick Corea, among others. We guitarists figured this out a little bit later but have made it a valuable tool in our harmonic vocabulary.

While quartal harmony certainly has great compositional and improvisational applications, the focus of this chapter will be its use in comping. You'll remember the term "comping by scale" from chapter 5. That really defines quartal harmony in comping situations perfectly. Instead of using a tertian-voiced structure (containing guide tones that relate to a specific chord type), we comp utilizing a stacked scale (creating multiple horizontal structures) in fourths that relates to the given chord type.

Let's say the given chord symbol is CMaj7. Play the stacked C Ionian (or "major") scale in figure 6.1 over a bass line on a CMaj7 chord. As you move from one quartal structure to another, the overall affect is an ebb and flow between tensions and releases to the basic chord tones (vertically speaking) contained in the chord scale.

Fig. 6.1. C Ionian Scale Stacked in Fourths

Notice that the chord built on C is unstable and ambiguous. This CMaj7 chord features a natural 11 instead of the more typical ♯11. It becomes "normalized" as we pass through the other structures from the stacked scale tones. Play this stacked scale for CMaj7, and you'll get the idea pretty quickly.

What makes this concept so valuable to us is the relationship between the modes derived from (in this case) the parent major scale and its respective chord associations. Most of us learn modes as a melodic source with which to improvise over particular chord types. In the basic tertiary chord/scale relationships, the chord tones are contained in the scale with which we improvise over the given chord. This creates a strong relationship between chord and scale.

But with quartal harmonies, the basic scale derivatives (modes) come from the primary scale (in the above example, Ionian) and their relationships to some basic chord types. These are very *basic* relationships. At this stage, all scales/modes are related from the scale's tonic (or starting note) to the chords based on their roots.

To review, here are the seven modes of the major scale and some basic chord relationships (see chapters 2 and 3), with examples from the key of C.

Degree	Scale and Chords	Example
I	**Ionian mode or major scale** used over Maj, Maj6, Maj7, Maj9, Maj13	**C Ionian or major scale** used over CMaj, CMaj6, CMaj7, CMaj9, CMaj13
II	**Dorian** used over min, −6, −7, −9, −11, −13	**D Dorian** used over D−, D−6, D−7, D−9, D−11, D−13
III	**Phrygian** used over 7sus4(♭9)	**E Phrygian** used over E7sus4(♭9)
IV	**Lydian** used over Maj7(♯11), Maj9(♯11), Maj13(♯11)	**F Lydian** used over FMaj7(♯11), FMaj7(9,♯11), FMaj7(♯11,13)
V	**Mixolydian** used over 7, 9, 11, 13, 7sus4, 9sus4, 13sus4 (dominant 7 chords)	**G Mixolydian** used over G7, G9, G11, G13, G7sus4, Gsus4(9), Gsus4(13)
VI	**Aeolian** used over min, −♭6, −7 with ♭13, −9, −11	**A Aeolian** used over A−, A−♭6, A−7(♭13), A−7(9), A−7(11)
VII	**Locrian** used over −7♭5, −7♭5(11)	**B Locrian** used over B−7♭5, B−7♭5(11)

Fig. 6.2. Scale Degrees, Modes, and Chords

With the harmonized scale in fourths, we'll revisit the above chord/scale relationships horizontally. We've already tried C Ionian in fourths, over CMaj7; now let's try it over D−7 (notes of the C Ionian from D to D), which creates a harmonized Dorian chord scale. Also, try D Dorian over G7, which creates a 7sus4 quality.

Fig. 6.3. D Dorian Chord Scale in Fourths

You'll notice that the preceding example is only the C Ionian mode, and its structures, starting from D.

As you'll remember from chapter 2, when creating modes of a scale, there are basically two methods of reckoning the notes. Let's review this material before employing quartal structures.

One is to start from the parent scale and its key signature. With this method, one just applies the parent scale's key signature to the sequence of tones that start from one of the parent scale's notes. Notice that the preceding modes from the major scale are given Roman numerals (I, II, III, IV, etc.). Starting from the third degree (III) of a major scale, and keeping the sequence of seven notes diatonic to that scale, creates a Phrygian mode. Beginning with C major and playing E, F, G, A, B, C, D, E creates an E Phrygian scale. E Phrygian is derived from C major/Ionian.

The other method for constructing modes is called parallel, and scales/ modes are generated via a number sequence (or formula). These numbers refer to the notes of a hypothetical major scale that have been altered to utilize the formula for a given scale type. For instance, the formula numerically for Phrygian mode is: 1, ♭2, ♭3, 4, 5, ♭6, ♭7. The notes spelled alphabetically (from E) would be: E, F, G, A, B, C, D, E. The "flatted," or in this case "naturaled," notes of the E Phrygian scale result from lowering the 2, 3, 6, and 7 degrees of an E major scale (E, F♯, G♯, A, B, C♯, D♯). Either way you look at it, you need to have good control of manipulating major scales and their key signatures to create parallel or derivative scales. By the way, so far we're just talking about major scales. Later we'll look at other primary seven-tone scales, such as melodic minor, harmonic minor, and harmonic major, that act as parent scales, generating their own unique set of modes. But, before you try the other scales, start with the major scales stacked quartally and played against all the chords/ modes listed above. Then try transposing these relationships to other keys and chord roots.

Don't let the theory speak turn you off. It's important to have control of the terminology, but in the end, your ear and tactile sense (muscle memory) will take over.

Quartal chord shapes are basically built around five shapes that use four notes. (Try paring these shapes down to three notes and also adding on to get five-note forms.) The four-note versions are easily played on four consecutive strings, from the fifth string or fourth string. All examples are built on the pitch C.

They look like this from the fifth string:

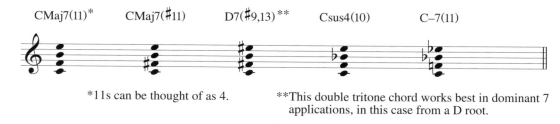

*11s can be thought of as 4.   **This double tritone chord works best in dominant 7
                                        applications, in this case from a D root.

Fig. 6.4. Types of Fourth Voicings

The major scale shapes include all but the one in the middle. Notice that
all the chords are made up of perfect fourths or tritones. Other scales, such
as harmonic minor and harmonic major, necessitate the spelling of the occasional diminished fourth interval. This will alter some shapes of the basic five
above (to keep structures diatonic to the scale). Some familiar tertian grips will
result, but you can still "think" in fourths. Here are the four seven-tone scales
we use in Berklee's guitar curriculum, harmonized in fourths. All examples are
built on C.

Ionian or Major Scale

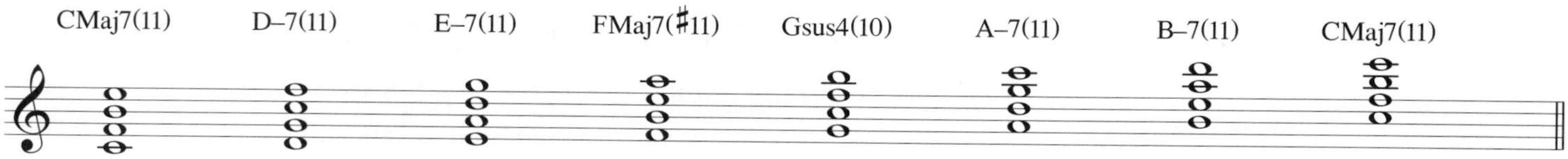

Melodic Minor Scale

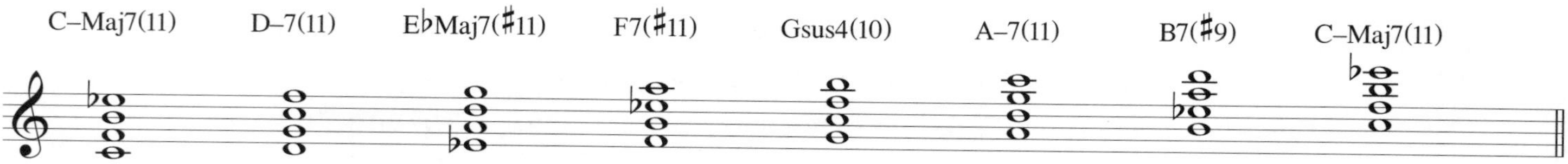

Harmonic Minor Scale

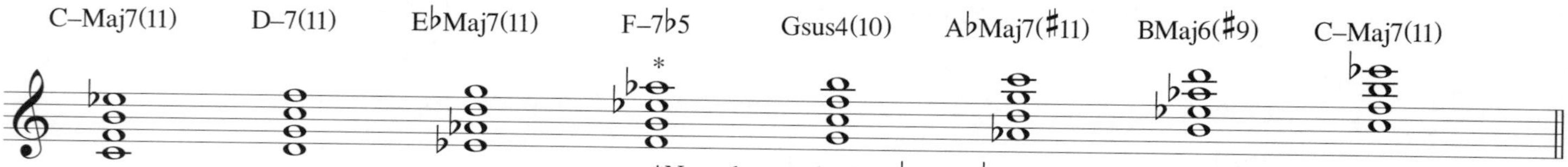

*Note that on the Fm7♭5, the ♭5 is spelled enharmonically as B (not C♭).

Harmonic Major Scale

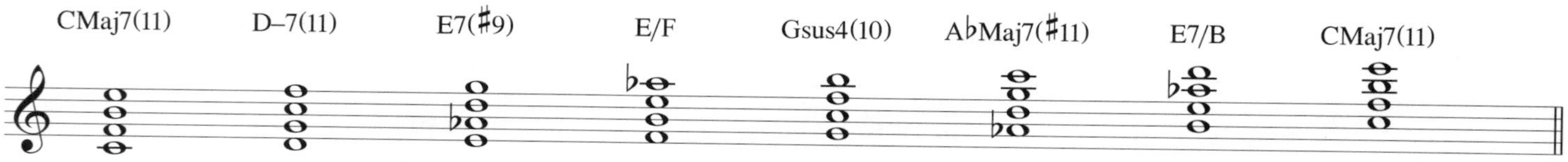

Fig. 6.5. Four Seven-Tone Scales in Fourths

As you can see, analysis gets pretty complex when using harmonic major/minor. I've broken it down to some familiar tertian structures or slash chords in those cases. Each of the preceding harmonized scales can be played over any chord contained in that scale's resultant harmonies. For instance, record an E7(♯9) vamp, and play the C harmonic major harmonized in fourths over it. Try the scale from the E7(♯9) root (E to E), and start from other tones in the C scale, as well. This is a good place to begin, listening to the sounds generated from a harmonized scale over the individual chord types contained in the scale's resultant harmony. It's also a really big job with multiple choices of scales for many chord types. How do you organize this? As simply as possible! Start with the major scale (in multiple keys), exhaust its possibilities, and then move on to melodic minor, etc. It's also very important to gain perspective in usage by listening to some of the pianists I've already mentioned, as well as guitarists like Mike Stern, Charlie Hunter, and John Scofield, and especially listen to organist Larry Young. One thing you'll notice immediately is that these guys don't play the entire harmonized scale from beginning to end. Often, using just two or three structures from a "key of the moment" (and the "key" can change with each chord) does the trick. Pay attention to melodic voice leading, and the use of sequential melodic ideas that are harmonized.

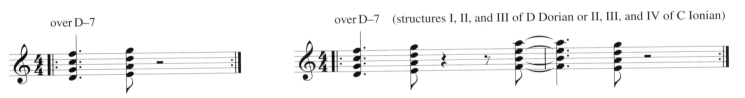

Fig. 6.6. Examples of Fourth Chord Comping

Now that we have some tools to work with, let's sum up how to get started:

1. Experiment with and imitate what you hear on recordings. Records such as Coltrane's *Complete 1961 Village Vangard Recordings* (with McCoy Tyner on piano) will give you lots of ideas to work with. Emulate the rhythms and number of structures being used in, for example, a four bar phrase. And while vamps are a very good place to begin, integrate your new vocabulary into cycles such as I VI II V and II V I. Then, try a jazz standard.

2. Try writing to develop workable ideas that you can recycle into other tunes.

3. Think context. These sounds tend to be modern in quality and fit very well with pentatonic language; for instance, check out McCoy. Later, as a deviation from the seven-tone scales that we're starting with, try stacking pentatonic, whole-tone, and other non-seven-tone scales. You'll come up with some very cool sounds! Remember, though, that these sounds might not be appropriate for older jazz styles. Use your ears, and study jazz styles by period to gain a sense of appropriate usage.

4. And lastly, even in a "fusion" or "modern jazz" context, you don't have to use fourth structures exclusively. Mixing tertian structures with quartal makes for a nice "pallet" of harmonic colors. The tertian chords will "nail down" the chord quality, while the quartal will be more ambiguous and achieve some nice passing chord movement. Here's an example of comping integrating both types into a standard jazz progression ("Stella by Starlight"). All fourth chord structures will be derived from major scales/modes used in a "key of the moment" sense. Notice that the fourth chord segments are very obvious. Keep your own examples simple, too. Later, you can get more complex and rhythmically daring. For right now, get the concepts down. Analyze, borrow, listen, and integrate them into your own versions! All chord symbols are broken down to basic structures. You do the analysis.

Jazz Progression 1

Track 15 - w/Guitar
Track 16 - w/o Guitar

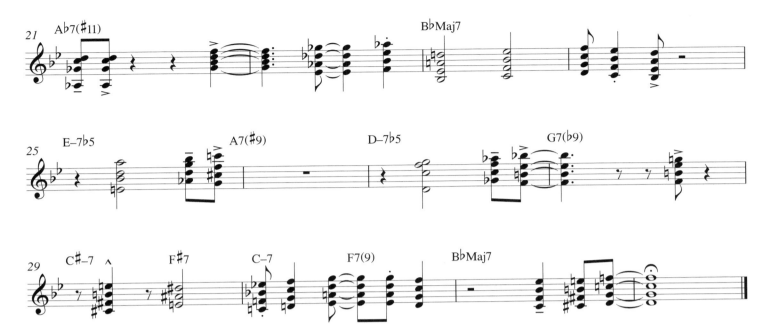

Fig. 6.7. Standard Jazz Progression Etude

MAKE IT REAL!
Try your own written versions on the bop tunes you're preparing!

Form and Progression

STRUCTURAL ORGANIZATION OF TUNES

Jazz tunes and most kinds of music have an underlying structural skeleton comprised of sections that make up what we call "form." Classical musicians have utilized this concept for hundreds of years, and virtually all pop, rock, theater music, etc. make use of form, too. For jazz musicians, form is very important because we improvise over harmonies in the form structure of the tunes we play. Don't mix up arrangement with form. They are connected, but absolutely different. So how do we define form? Maybe the best explanation would be an example, the twelve bar blues.

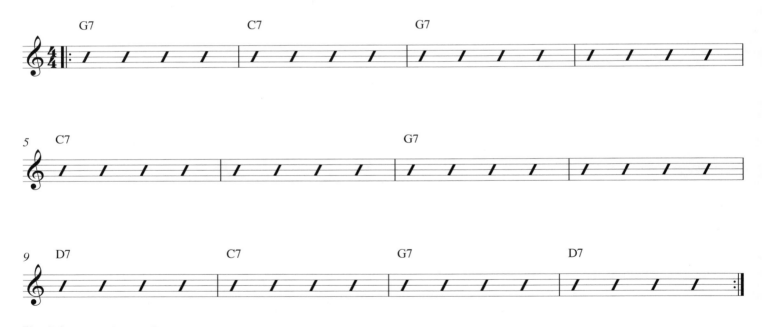

Fig. 7.1. Basic Blues Form

This basic blues progression has been the template for countless songs in every genre. From R&B/rock tunes like "Johnny B. Goode" to a jazz head like "Chicken Shack," this repeating, underlying 12-bar structure is used to build the song and performance. How do chords relate to the form? The term "harmonic rhythm" refers to the duration of the chords related to the pulse of a meter. For instance, the first chord (G7) lasts for four beats before moving to the C7 chord in bar 2, which also lasts for four beats before returning to the G7 chord. The way these chords progress through a 12-bar cycle and then repeat is an example of form.

There are many different forms that are *standard* in the jazz repertoire. After blues, probably the most frequently recurrent jazz form is AABA, where each letter represents a section of the chord progression. An example of a tune using AABA form is "I Got Rhythm." "Rhythm changes" is a 32-bar form consisting of three similar "A" sections comprised of eight bars each, with a contrasting "B" section known as the bridge, or relief. The "B" section is also made up of eight bars. The chords can vary in different versions of rhythm changes, but this AABA form with its eight bar sections totaling thirty-two bars is the "norm." Here's an example of rhythm changes.

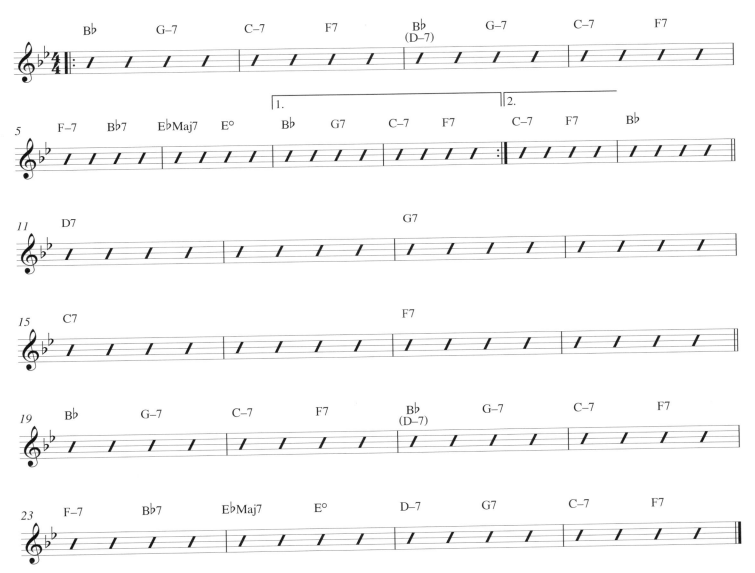

Fig. 7.2. Rhythm Changes

Many jazz tunes use this form, with different harmonic progressions. Some well-known examples are "There Is No Greater Love," "Softly as in a Morning Sunrise," and "Misty."

The AABA form can be extended to sixty-four bars, as well, such as Cole Porter's "Love for Sale." Many tunes extend sections of the AABA form with the number of bars used, like in "Alone Together," with its 14-bar A sections (the bridge in this tune is eight bars and the last eight A section is reduced to eight bars). A tune like "I'll Remember April" uses ABA form with 16-bar sections. Another form, that I'll call the double sixteen, is also very common. Tunes like "On Green Dolphin Street," "But Not for Me," and "There Will Never Be Another You" are good examples. This form also can be extended, as in the case of Sonny Rollins' tune "Airegin." It might be helpful to designate this form as AA' (prime, meaning, a variation of A), since the first A is twenty bars in duration and the second A is sixteen.

Many modern tunes have forms of varying length in total bar numbers, like Horace Silver's "Peace," which is ten bars in length. It's a series of short progressions that repeat in a 10-bar form—no A or B sections.

Forms can be extended to include more sections and incorporate interludes and *tags* (ending vamps that repeat). These forms are made up in many ways. The main thing for us to recognize at this point is how they fit into our performance as jazz guitarists. Let's recap:

- Forms are the underlying harmonic structure of tunes as related to time.

- Segments of these harmonies can be organized into sections, and the sections can be organized into song forms that can be formulaic and related to many common tunes.

- Forms also can be comprised of widely varying numbers of bars and juxtapositions of sections.

Typically, as improvisers, we play the melody of a tune, then solo on the chords that support the melody of that tune. Song forms are comprised of chord progressions. So this is a good time to look at progression and how chord progression relates to song form. A given chord can *progress* to any other chord, hence the term "progression." Progressions frequently can be analyzed in terms of relating to a common scale (diatonic harmonies) where a series of chords are analyzed relative to a parent scale and key. Roman numerals are used to relate the chord to scale degrees, and major, minor, dominant 7, etc., are attached to qualify the type of chord. The diatonic seventh chords in the key of C major would be:

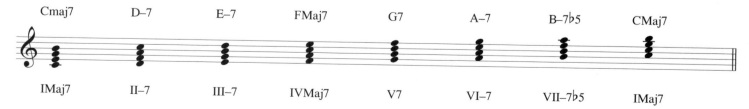

Fig. 7.3. Diatonic Seventh Chords in C Major

A typical diatonic chord progression used in making up a tune would be I VI II V. In the key of C, these would be the chords:

Fig. 7.4. I VI II V Progression in C Major

Chord progressions can be made up of non-diatonic harmonies, as well. These may include chords made up of notes that don't relate to a given scale/key diatonically but still incorporate a diatonic root progression.

Fig. 7.5. I VI II V Progression in C Major with Non-Diatonic Chords

Chord progressions can relate to major or minor tonalities but utilize non-diatonic roots as well as chord tones not found in the key/scale. This example can be analyzed as I ♭III ♭VI ♭II in C major.

Fig. 7.6. Non-Diatonic Root Progression

There are additional classifications of harmony, such as nonfunctional, etc. It takes a lot of time and experience to learn all this information. Our goal here is to grasp the application of some basic relationships of this theory to music making. And this really gets us back to tunes. Progression of chords fits in with the concept of form. Many songs feature *standard* chord changes combined with common forms. Examples of some standard chord progressions that make up portions of standard tunes include:

II–7	V7		
II–7	V7	I	
I	VI–7	II–7	V7
III–7	VI–7	II–7	V7
I	IV7	V7	I

They can be related to several different types of minor scales, such as melodic, Aeolian, or harmonic:

II–7♭5	V7(alt)		
II–7♭5	V7(alt)	I–7	
I–7	VI–7♭5	II–7♭5	V7(alt)
♭IIIMaj7	VI–7♭5	II–7♭5	V7
I–7	IV–7	V7(alt)	I–7

These diatonic root progressions can feature non-diatonic harmonies and be applied to major or minor keys:

II7	V7		
II7	V7	I	
I	VI7	II–7	V7
III7	VI7	II7	V7
I	IV–7	V7	I

♭VI	V7(alt)	I–7	
II–7♭5	♭VI	V7(alt)	I–7
I–7	VI7	II7	V7(alt)
♭III–7	♭VI7	II7	V7
I–7	IV–7	V7(alt)	I–7

This is just a small sample of typical standard tune harmonic progressions. These examples feature diatonic-root progressions, but there are plenty that don't, such as figure 7.6. (*Diatonic* means that the notes come from the scale.) Progressions can be mixed together within a section or sections of a tune. Or they might move between relative major and minor keys (a common scheme), like the progression in the first eight bars of another progression, used in "Autumn Leaves" and other tunes.

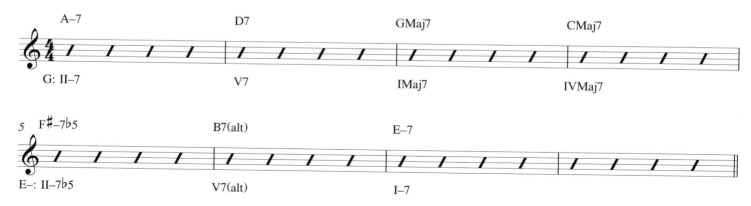

Fig. 7.7. Progression Analysis

Progressions can move through what are called "key of the moment" sections, like this excerpt used in tunes such as "Have You Met Miss Jones," which features II–7 V7 I in several keys.

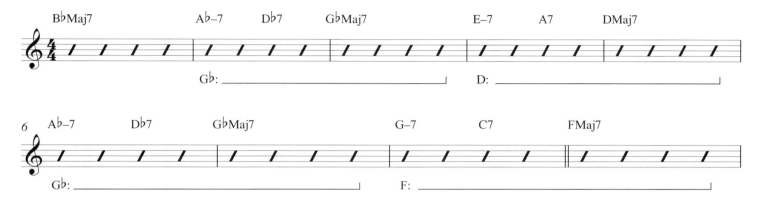

Fig. 7.8. Key of the Moment Progressions

There are infinite variations, and in-depth harmonic analysis is a subject beyond the scope of this chapter. But you can start to notice how form and progression work together.

And, most important, you'll be able to learn more tunes, which in turn become vehicles for your soloing, comping, chord solos, etc. We need repertoire to interact with other musicians, but learning tunes can be difficult for inexperienced players. The uninitiated tend to think about one chord after the next, like this: FMaj7 to G7 to G–7 to C7, etc. When you learn to look at the bigger picture of form and progression, it becomes easier to retain these tunes, not to mention being able to play them in multiple keys. Many tunes also share portions of the same common standard progressions and forms, making them easier to remember. For instance, here's a progression I II7 II–7 V7 in AABA form.

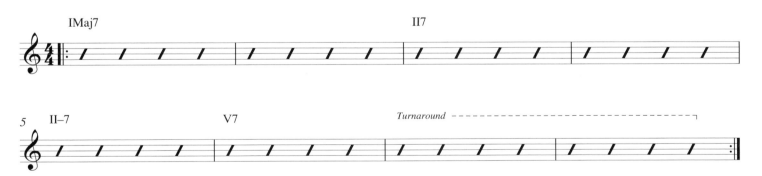

Fig. 7.9. Standard Jazz Tune Progression

These eight bars make up the "A" sections of the following standard AABA form tunes:

"Take the A Train" (use a ♭5 for relating to melody on the II7 chord)

"Watch What Happens"

"Jersey Bounce"

"The Girl from Ipanema"

The *turnaround* section is found universally in jazz tunes. It is usually two bars in length (though it can be longer or shorter), and it literally turns around the end of a section with a series of chords to repeat that section again, or to repeat and begin a form again. Think of the turnaround as a modular idea. It can be transplanted to many different situations. Here are some examples of turnarounds. Can you analyze them, assign Roman numerals, and play them in several keys? Try plugging these into the turnaround bars of "Take the A Train."

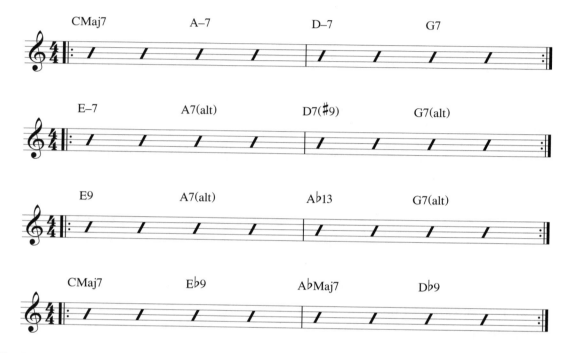

Fig. 7.10. Examples of Turnarounds

It's a good idea to analyze tunes and keep a list of them organized by form and notable progressions. Keep track of tunes that you hear, that are called at sessions, or that you study in class. Practice your repertoire by learning and playing in meter:

1. The melody

2. The chord progression

3. At least some of the melody harmonized

MAKE IT REAL!

Try learning a tune every week. Do some research on compiling tunes that other musicians frequently perform, tunes that you may be called upon to perform at an audition, tunes that you like, and tunes that are varied in nature (swing, Latin, bossa, 4/4 3/4 6/8 12/8 5/4, *etc.*). Maintain and practice your repertoire daily. In a year you'll have fifty-two tunes together!

PART II

LET'S GET PLAYING

CHAPTER 8

Roles: Walking Bass Lines, Comping, Soloing

SOME THINGS TO CONSIDER

Before you start your playing sessions, it's a good idea to consider your roles as a guitarist in a group. Simply put, the jobs are soloist, accompanist, and ensemble member—not necessarily in that order. If you're playing in a duo situation, obviously the lines blur a bit, but these are the ways we function as guitarists. And while we tend to be preoccupied with soloing, the accompanist and ensemble roles are just as important.

Musicians interface collectively on a musical vehicle that could be a jazz tune interpreted by a trio, an arrangement of a tune scored for a large ensemble, and even "free" collective improvisation on a theme, a scale, or just a mood. Listening to recordings from all periods of jazz history is essential. The answers to many questions become obvious in the recordings. Listening to recordings should be a part of your daily routine!

We'll approach our playing from a tune-based reality in a small group setting. Once musicians get together to play, the first question is usually: "What do you want to play?" Once you pick a tune, it's time to play. At this point, many will start by reading a "lead sheet" of a jazz or standard tune. Unless you're playing a contemporary tune with more concise notation (like a composer's approved edition), most lead sheets are basic in their representation of the melody and harmony. Take a look at a jazz standard, like "All the Things You Are" in a jazz "fakebook," and you'll see that the melody is very basic and that most of the chords are just basic seventh chords. This is where listening to a version of the song by a jazz artist who you like is critical for reference. You'll notice that the artist(s) will embellish the melody, add nuances such as slides and bends, and rhythmically alter what you're seeing on the lead sheet. Harmonies in the accompaniment will feature use of tensions, substitute chords, and rhythms not notated on the lead sheet. So, before you attempt to play, it's a good idea to do your "homework" by listening to recorded performances of a given tune, and check out the traditions of how the tune can be played—and there will be a lot of variation. Once you've got this first step together, you need to learn how to function in the roles of accompanist and soloist.

Consider that many guitarists begin by jamming with another guitarist. Guitarists are a "curiously clannish bunch" (as Gene Lees said in his album notes to *Movin' Wes*), and there are a lot of us guitarists, which is convenient for gaining playing experience. Or, we might start by soloing over play-along tracks we create ourselves, perhaps by looping chord progressions on sampling boxes, etc. Just comping chords by ourselves to back up another instrumentalist can sound a little empty, and the timing can be quirky and ambiguous.

Bass lines can help solidify the time feel of our accompaniment. In addition, they are a staple duo-playing ingredient and have a history in the jazz guitar tradition of greats like Joe Pass. Plus they're fun to play! So, we will start our discussion of accompaniment with bass lines.

WALKING BASS LINES FOR GUITARIST: REALITY CHECK!

Bass lines are an excellent means of improving your musicianship on the guitar. Learning to improvise/write bass lines offers several benefits.

A good bass line:

1. Provides a solid, swinging accompaniment for duo playing and for the creation of practice play-along recordings.

2. Helps to develop an intuitive sense of tunes' harmonic rhythm and progressions (chord changes) by orienting to the bass line.

3. Incorporates many "basic" improvisational concepts and fundamental musical building blocks, such as chord tone outlining/scales with chromaticism and use of sequence, to mention just a few tools that are essential for improvising in the jazz/fusion idioms.

While all the above is true, the main focus here is to play with other musicians and prepare your own practice materials, so let's look at how to create some bass lines.

Step 1. Root and 5th Orientation

Begin with a quarter note "walking" root and 5th bass line, utilizing primarily the first and third fingers. Play the root and 5th of each chord where time permits. Connect the chord changes, experimenting with different string groups, but stay on the low side in the bass register. You should be able to do this with any progression at sight, in meter. Alter any fifths as directed, such as ♭5. (Often, a ♯5 in the chord symbol is really a ♭13, and the 5th in the bass line should be a natural 5; use your ear!) It is essential to have mastered your basic chord construction in twelve keys.

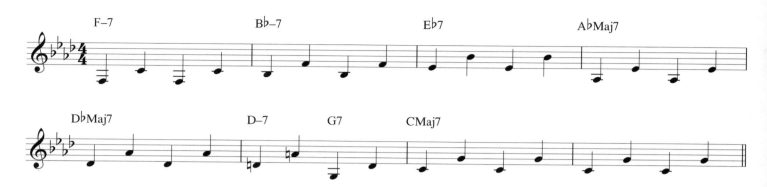

Fig. 8.1. Root and 5th Bass Line

Step 2. Root and 5th with Chromatic Approach

When the chord changes, play the root, then the root or fifth can be approached chromatically from above or below. Work backwards from the root, as in the following examples. Temporary rule: play the root where the chord changes.

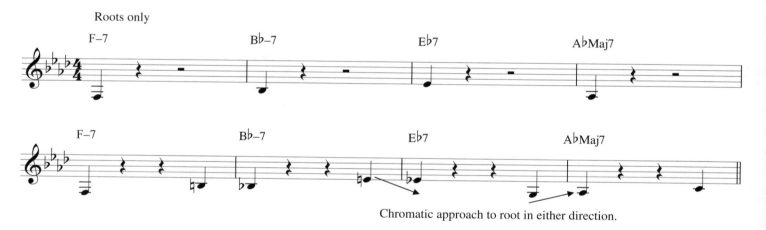

Chromatic approach to root in either direction.

Fig. 8.2. Roots Only, Then Chromatically Approached

Fig. 8.3. Approaching 5th and Root

When playing two changes per bar, there is only time to play the roots where the chord changes and connect with chromatics above or below: practice this vamp with all approaches from above, then all from below, then mixing in both directions.

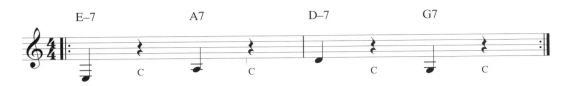

Fig. 8.4. Two Changes per Bar

You would play only the root in this example with four changes in the bar.

Fig. 8.5. Four Changes per Bar

For the time being, we're still using the "when chord changes, play the root" rule. The first eight bars of our bass line might look like this:

Fig. 8.6. Root/Fifth Bass Line with Chromatics

This method works okay, but you'll notice the line is a little "jerky" and "robotic" sounding due to the resulting ♭6 and tritone intervals created by following the approaches to the root and fifth method. To create a smoother line, let's go on to the next big building blocks for bass lines: scales and scales with chromatics.

Step 3. Scales and Scales with Chromatics

Any basic chord scale intended for bass line application can be used by itself or enhanced by the use of chromatics.

Fig. 8.7. G Mixolydian Chord Scale

G Mixolydian with added chromatics

Fig. 8.8. Mixolydian with Added Chromatics

Start with major, Dorian, and Mixolydian, and try adding chromatic connectors between scale steps 2–3, 4–5, and ♭7–1. Sometimes, when chromatic connectors are added to a scale, they can also be analyzed as a chord tone or scale tone approach, as shown in this example.

Fig. 8.9. Scales Using Chromatics

Too much scale with chromaticism can get a bit too smooth and wishy-washy. So, there is yet another main ingredient that adds diversity.

Step 4. Chord Tone Outline by Triads/Seventh Chord

Fig. 8.10. Chord Tone Outlines

Too much chord tone outlining, especially triadic, can make you feel like you're caught in a bad Elvis movie! But, there's still great potential for musicality through manipulation of the chord tones. The chord outline doesn't always have to spell from the root up: 1 3 5 7. Try 1 5 3 7, 1 7 5 3, etc. With the inversions of chord tones available, you can see the potential for where non-roots on chord changes become possible.

Steps 2, 3, and 4 are the basic components of bass line construction.

You'll find, though, that frequent juxtaposition of the different components is necessary to keep things interesting. The following is an example of the three ingredients at work in our bass line. Notice that scale fragments such as 1, 2, 3, 5, or even a plain scale without chromatics, can be used to connect chords effectively.

Jazz Progression 2

Track 17 - Slow w/Guitar
Track 18 - Slow w/o Guitar
Track 19 - Fast w/Guitar
Track 20 - Fast w/o Guitar

Fig. 8.11. Bass Line with Steps 1 to 4

Step 5. Variation of Basic Elements

You can get a lot more musical mileage out of the basic building devices by applying these variations to your bass lines.

    1. Sequence. Here's a simple scale fragment plugged into a minor blues.

Fig. 8.12. Sequence

    2. Doubled notes. Check out bassist Charlie Haden for good examples of this device.

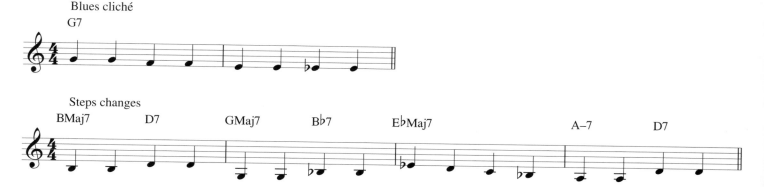

Fig. 8.13. Doubled Notes

    3. Large interval skips by 10th, 9th, octave, and 7th.

Fig. 8.14. Skips

    4. The secret weapon: percussive/rhythmic effects. Up until this point, all of our bass line generators have been pitch-oriented. Another way to create interest, variation, and rhythmic "drive" utilizes what I call the "flam." Think like a jazz drummer improvising reactive "hits" using the snare drum. The "abstractions," as some drummers call them, are reactions to the music and also a way to heat up the interplay between the performers. We don't really relate the pitch of a snare drum to a song's tonality or a chord change, and in the same way, we can use rhythmic effects *percussively* on the guitar using muted open strings and chord shapes without affecting the music in a negative way.

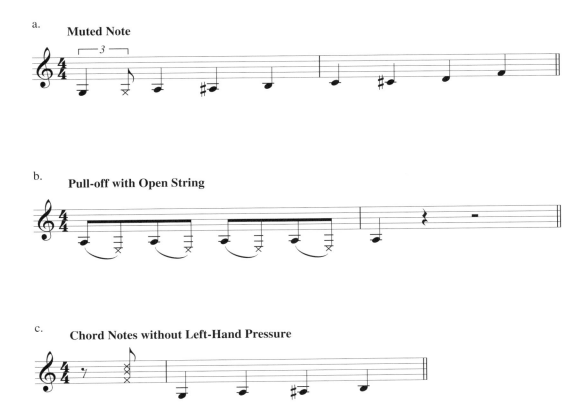

Fig. 8.15. Percussive Effects

Bassist Ron Carter is a master of these effects on double bass. Check out the way he uses them! We guitarists benefit from these rhythmic effects by "disguising" the elements we're using to create our lines. And you get drive, as well as the "surprise" factor. Try to use these effects randomly so they're unpredictable.

We now have the basic elements to make good bass lines. Of course, these ideas are fairly theory-oriented. To make these elements come alive musically, you need to listen to examples of the art of bass playing by great double-bass players like Ron Carter, Paul Chambers, Percy Heath, Niels-Henning Ørsted Pedersen, and Ray Brown. Check out modern players of the electric bass like Jeff Andrews, Jeff Berlin, Jaco Pastorius, and so on. See what Joe Pass and Charlie Hunter do with bass lines on their guitars. *Transcribe!* Find out what's going on with your ears!

Write! Practice writing bass lines on tunes. Start with the blues or a simple jazz standard like "Summertime," and scrutinize your written lines for good content. *Use the eraser as much as the lead in your pencil! Play what you write,* work on the groove, and "feel." Try playing a line only on one string, then two, then three, and *sing what you play*! You'll be surprised what a great "orientation exercise" this is. Try to relate these ideas to your improvisations. One last idea: Listen to jazz organ players like Larry Young. Organists tend to play what I think of as functional bass lines—while swinging their tails off! We guitarists can learn a lot from them.

COMPING

The term comping is short for "accompaniment," or "to complement." Either way you look at it, we're performing a vital rhythm section function for chord playing instruments that you need to get together. This could easily be a book in itself. But, let's explore some essential comping concepts. All examples will be in 4/4 meter, and we're concentrating only on jazz swing feel.

A comper supplies chords for a soloist to play over, provides the chords to a group that supports the harmonies of a given tune, or vamps, playing with improvised rhythms. The comper interacts with all the members of the group in a communal, conversational way. The comper utilizes chord choices that compliment a performance harmonically, rhythmically, and asthetically. While all of this obviously takes a lot of time and skill to get together, we'll approach the basics by using our chord knowledge base with three rhythmic ideas:

1. Chords played on the beat

2. Chords played off the beat

3. Chords played with polyrhythms/tuplets

Here's an example of a blues using four-to-the-bar chords, like Herb Ellis.

Track 21 - w/Guitar
Track 22 - w/o Guitar

Blues in G

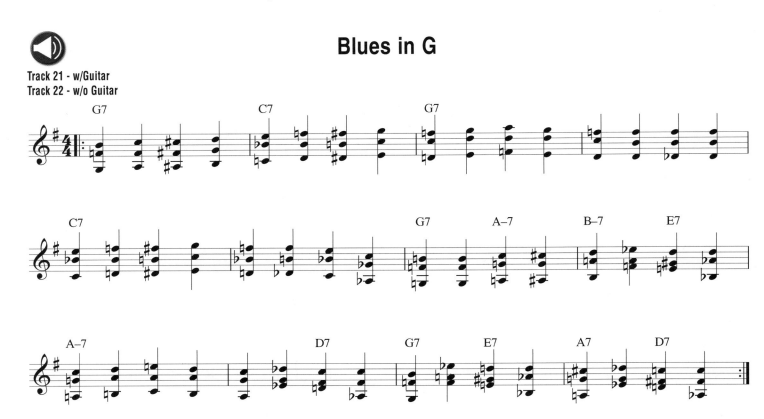

Fig. 8.16. G Blues, Four to the Bar

You'll notice that many of these chords are moved into chromatically. This is very standard practice. Just about any chord can be approached chromatically. All of the primary chords feature the guide tones along with a bass note that is usually a root, 3rd, or a 5th. Notice, as well, that the bottom of the chords form a bass line.

Blues in G: Walking Bass

Track 23 - w/Guitar
Track 24 - w/o Guitar

Fig. 8.17. Bass Line from Blues in G

Try playing the bass line with some of the notes randomly harmonized, and you have a typical duo playing session comping tool: the chords with bass line scenario. The chords can be added on the beat or off the beat, like this:

Blues in G: Walking Bass with Chords

Track 25 - w/Guitar
Track 26 - w/o Guitar

Fig. 8.18. Walking Bass with Chords

Try the bass line with your own chords, and add the percussive effects previously discussed. Try not to harmonize the bass constantly in the same place, like beat 1. It's too predictable. As useful as this is for duo playing and recording your own play-alongs, take care when playing chords and bass lines in a group setting. Many players in a big band setting will play rhythm guitar using voicings like figure 8.16 and drive the bass player bananas! You can certainly use some of this concept when playing four-to-the-bar rhythm, but the secret to co-existing with the bassist, in this style, is to play the bottom strings percussively, and bring out the middle note on your chord voicing, frequently on the "D" string. The trick is to finger a standard chord, but muffle the bottom note and maybe not even play the top one, even though your finger is on it. Think like this:

Fig. 8.19. One-Note Chords

The concept is called "one-note chords." Elevated to an art form by Freddie Green of the Count Basie Orchestra, this device effectively adds rhythm "shump," while staying out of the way of the bass player. A couple of great contemporary players who use this technique are Bucky Pizzarelli and his son John Pizzarelli. Check them out, and buy all their recordings!

OFF-THE-BEAT AND ANTICIPATED COMPING RHYTHMS

While playing bass lines with chords and four-to-the-floor rhythm styles can be very cool, they *tend* to be relegated to duo usage and swing band style playing—though never say never! Listen to Wes Montgomery playing four to the floor on "Satin Doll." In what was once termed "combo" style comping, we tend to use less four-to-the-floor playing and use more open improvised rhythms that react to the players we're comping for. For our purposes here, we'll again concentrate on 4/4 meter. Figure 8.20 is a good preparatory study to practice off-the-beat rhythms that anticipate downbeats. Each dot preceding a beat number represents an accented eighth note anticipating the coming beat. The eighth note should be played with a "swing feel" (♪♪ = ♪♪). Each line of four beats is a separate exercise.

•1	2	3	4
1	•2	3	4
1	2	•3	4
1	2	3	•4

Fig. 8.20. Anticipation Exercises

In notation, they look like this:

a. Anticipate Beat 1

b. Anticipate Beat 2

c. Anticipate Beat 3

d. Anticipate Beat 4

Fig. 8.21. Notated Anticipation Exercises

Take a standard tune, and practice rhythmically anticipating a target beat through the entire form. This is a good way to incorporate new chord vocabulary as you have a fair amount of time to get from one voicing to the next. An added bonus from playing chords off the beat is the way these rhythms support faster tempos. Long duration rhythms always on the beat can feel sluggish and weigh a tempo down. Off the beat hits help things move, leave space, and pop. Try playing a chorus of blues with all whole note duration chords played on the beat, and then play some short, off the beat hits. See the difference? Here's an example of choosing chord voicings on a blues progression and then anticipating only the first beat.

Blues in B♭: with Anticipations

Track 27 - w/Guitar
Track 28 - w/o Guitar

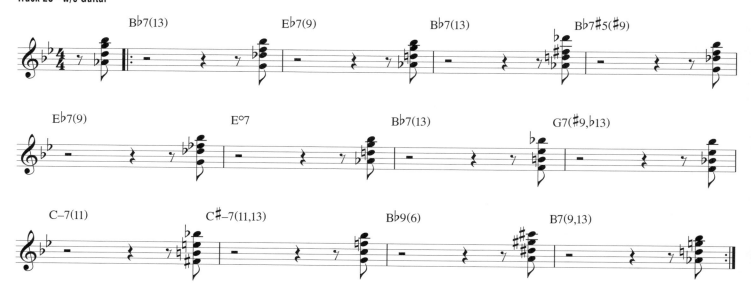

Fig. 8.22. Anticipations on 4+

When you've gone through all four possibilities (anticipating all four beats), combine two of them. Of course, you need two voicings now. You can repeat the same chord, or go to another voicing. If I played the previous blues with this concept, it might look like figure 8.23. (I'll use only anticipations to beats 1 and 3; you do the chord analysis!)

Blues in B♭: with Chord Anticipations

Track 29 - w/Guitar
Track 30 - w/o Guitar

Fig. 8.23. Anticipations to Beats 1 and 3

If you're getting the hang of playing chords off the beat, then you're ready to combine on-the-beat with off-the-beat. Let's take the previous example and make the first chord on the beat and the second off the beat.

Blues in B♭: On and Off the Beat

Track 31 - w/Guitar
Track 32 - w/o Guitar

Fig. 8.24. Combining On and Off the Beat

Once you see pretty clearly how this works, you can devise multitudes of examples yourself.

Polyrhythms are another typical comping device. They utilize an ongoing rhythmic cell that creates tension against the pulse of the meter. Polyrhythms can be comprised of rhythms that are on the beat and off the beat, as well as rhythmic figures like three against two (as in quarter note triplets). Polyrhythmic devices are widespread in jazz and are a long-term study. They are used in comping and soloing and with both chords and lines. Here's a brief example based on a dotted quarter note to give you an idea. Try to continue it over the previous blues progression.

Fig. 8.25. Polyrhythm Example

As with all types of devices used in jazz guitar comping, listening to the greats will give you insight on what to do in playing situations. I suggest that you listen to and transcribe examples of your favorite guitarists comping on recordings, then practice the ideas learned on tunes. For example: check out Wes Montgomery comping on "Smokin' at the Half Note." Try imitating some of the rhythms he comps on a tune of your choice. If you write down some of the rhythms and voice some chords, that would be great, but concentrate on just plugging in the comping ideas into other tunes by ear. Another great comper is Jim Hall. Try transcribing some of his comping from the Sonny Rollins recording, "The Bridge." Jim's choice of voicings and rhythmic interplay while comping is legendary and has influenced musicians around the globe.

PRESOLOING IDEAS AND INTERPRETATION OF JAZZ HEADS

As mentioned before, melodies and improvisations feature nuances such as slides, bends, drops, etc. These devices are sometimes "guitaristic" in nature but are more often derived from horns. While they can be described in words, I feel they are best incorporated by ear and from experience gained while playing with other musicians. The best way to get a sense of how to use these devices on your own is to play along with a recording. In particular, check out the interpretation of the head. Compared to a lead sheet version, chances are the artists' interpretation will be pretty different—especially on standard tunes and even from one recording to another of the same tune. Note the duration of pitches, embellishment, fills, and use of nuance. It can be very helpful to write down these versions, but it is even more important to be able to sing them and *then* play them on the guitar. Memorize and experiment with locations and fingerings. Try using some of the devices you've learned while interpreting other tunes you play.

TRANSCRIPTION AND SOLOING

Solo transcriptions are an important learning tool. This is a point of controversy among jazz musicians and educators, the argument against being that there is a risk of losing one's originality by copying others. While there are certainly some "clones" out there that totally mimic their heroes' guitar style, we can gain a lot of craft from playing along with recordings. The main benefit is linking ideas on the fingerboard. Along with all the scales, arpeggios, and other ingredients available for improvising comes confusion about how to put these elements together. When playing transcriptions by master players, we get into the head of those players and look at how they put their ideas together. When we finger and practice the transcription up to tempo, we gain knowledge about the content used, phrasing, and linkage on the fingerboard. We also learn to use nuance and gain the subtleties of articulation by playing along with recordings. This last factor, articulation, is an important element in making solo ideas work. There are some excellent books on the market that explore this content. They use written pieces marked with accents, long tones, and phrase markings that represent visually how a jazz player articulates and phrases. But like learning a language, repetition and study of phrases by ear is what gets you speaking. If you can play a piece along with a recording you solve technical and linkage issues *while* you assimilate the articulation intuitively by repetition! This is a time honored method and tradition in learning to play jazz. Gerry Mulligan wrote a bop tune called "Nights at the Turntable"—obviously autobiographical in nature! Wes Montgomery learned how to play guitar by copying Charlie Christian's solos verbatim. I had the privilege of studying with Charlie Banacos for almost twenty-three years, and transcription was a big part of the lessons—always!

With all of the improv concepts we'll explore in this book, finding examples of their usage is a big help in making them manifest on the guitar. Initially, playing transcribed solos, or even just passages from a solo, really helps to get us playing. We are forced to make decisions about where to locate an idea and how to execute it. After we imitate in the tradition, we can create our own variations, organize our own preferences regarding location and technique, and follow our own vibe.

MAKE IT REAL!

Everything in this book needs to be applied to tunes. Tunes are the vehicles that musicians use to communicate and perform with. Whether you're into mainstream, world, or fusion jazz, an active repertoire of tunes is a real necessity. Try applying the information presented here to tunes on a daily basis. Compile a list of tunes that are commonly played by jazz musicians. Learn some blues heads, some rhythm changes heads, and some common standard tunes by memory, and if possible, in different keys. After that, the more bop heads you learn, the better!

CHAPTER 9

Navigating Changes: Linear Improv Concepts

CHORD OUTLINES AND CHROMATIC APPROACHES

Making changes, getting "inside" the chords, playing with vertical content—no matter how you put it, this is every aspiring jazz guitarist's goal, and it's difficult to achieve. Why is this? The overwhelming amount of published material makes it difficult for many students to choose a starting point for study and to understand navigational concepts for organizing the fingerboard.

Many guitarists begin their linear improv studies with scales, which is fine. After all, the chords we're trying to improvise over are in the scales. Chord/scale theory, right? Scales are a great source of improv material. But it's easier, initially, to get "inside" the chords by orienting towards chord tone content instead of scales as an improv generator. I'd rather play chord content like this:

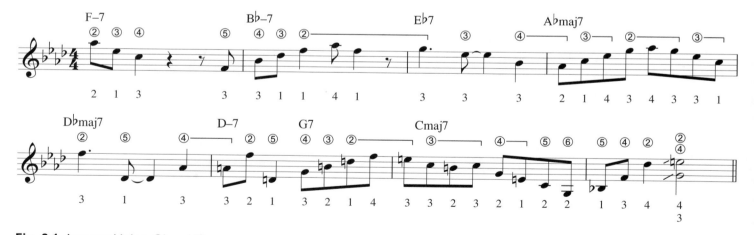

Fig. 9.1. Improv Using Chord Tones

It's easier than trying to jam scales into the time allotted for each chord.

Fig. 9.2. Jammin' the Scales

Scales, by nature, are long and even, so a lot of us start out trying to run long lines of them over changes when improvising. Chord content, however, can be triadic or outline low-degree seventh chords, so initially there are fewer notes to deal with (three and four respectively), and then we can relate to chord shapes on the fingerboard we may already know when playing chord outlines. We'll look at some ways to utilize scales in the next chapter, but first, let's narrow our focus to chord content.

Chord outlines can be pretty dull, especially if consistently played from the root up. Connecting inversions of different outlines and varying direction of the lines helps, but the sound can be very "inside." This is where the use of chromaticism comes in. Chromatics add interest when mixed into a chord tone line. This is one of the hallmarks of bop improvisation: outlines with chromaticism. The boppers used chromatics in scale lines, too, as well as other devices, but let's focus on chord outlines with chromatics.

This is where many of us have trouble navigating the fingerboard. How do we organize chromatics within the chord outlines? Does chromaticism come from the chromatic scale? And how do we mix the two elements together? Joe Pass was very fond of saying, "Where there's a chord, there's a line." Joe would use an approach like the following.

1. Take a simple scale fingering.

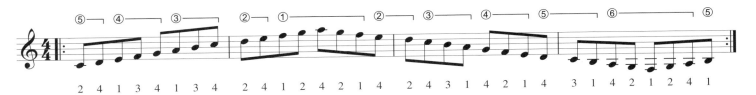

Fig. 9.3. C Major Scale

2. Play a chord like CMaj7(9), that had its chord tones in the scale shape.

Fig. 9.4. CMaj7(9) Chord

3. Play the chord's arpeggio out of the scale fingering.

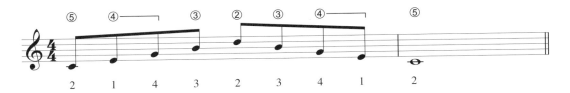

Fig. 9.5. CMaj9 Arpeggio

4. Then proceed to make a jazz line out of the chord outline and adding chromatics.

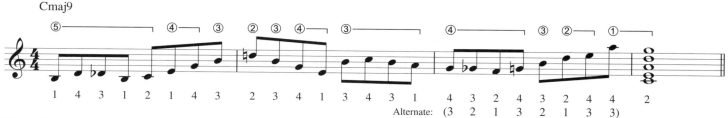

Fig. 9.6. Jazz Line on CMaj9

Sometimes, there were a couple of passing scale tones, too! It is easy to see the relationship between the scale, arpeggio, and chord shape, but it can take a long time to figure out how to organize the chromatic notes. What gradually becomes clear is that the chromatics are *between* the notes of the low chord degrees (1, 3, 5, 7). Navigationally, the approaches needed to be on the same string as the target chord tone. Here's the way to organize the chromatics.

Fig. 9.7. The Twelve Chromatic Approaches

All the above chromatic examples resolve into the pitch C, but it could be any chord tone on any type of chord. What is important is the distance, direction, and amount of chromatics in relation to the chord tone. You can make a great bop line exercise out of low degree outlines mixed with varying amounts of chromatics. Start with a two-octave arpeggio using a couple of different fingerings. One in position, one diagonal, for instance.

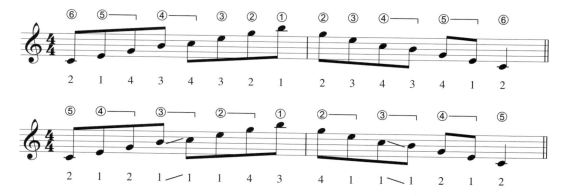

Fig. 9.8. Two Fingerings for a CMaj7 Arpeggio

The example in figure 9.8 is CMaj7, but the arpeggio could be any chord outline. Notice the high note only goes to the seventh of the chord. You can use any fingering that feels good to you, *but the approach note and its target tone should be on the same string.*

Now, start your exercises by adding one of the chromatic approaches to the outline, like this example of a one-half-step approach above the root. Start the line on or off the beat, whatever feels good.

Fig. 9.9. One-Half-Step Approach above the Root of CMaj7

Then, to the third of the chord:

Fig. 9.10. One-Half-Step Approach above the Third of CMaj7

Then, to the fifth of the chord:

Fig. 9.11. One-Half-Step Approach above the Fifth of CMaj7

And, finally, to the seventh of the chord:

Fig. 9.12. One-Half-Step Approach above the Seventh of CMaj7

Note that the approach in the last example is a chord tone as well as an approach. This results in a doubling of the note C as the arpeggio descends. Continue your exercises in twelve keys, using both fingerings to all four chord tones on the major seventh chords. Then, use the same half step above approach on the major 7♯5 chord, major 7♭5, etc., repeating the previous procedure until you go through all eleven chord types.

This has the potential to be very time consuming! If you look at the math: twelve approaches x eleven chord types x four chord tones x twelve keys = 6,336 exercises! And, don't forget two fingerings 6,336 x 2 = 12,672 exercises! Why would you take the time to do this? This is an immersion exercise.

Constant repetition helps burn these moves into your subconscious, where motion becomes auto-intuitive. Only extensive repetition accomplishes this. This also forces you to make decisions about fingering and orientation, which is great, and no one does them exactly the same way.

Try to sing what you play. A word of warning, however: move from side-to-side into the chord shapes, and keep the chromatics on the same string as the target chord tone. Play loose, and get used to the movement. Move and avoid stretching. It's better for the phrasing quality, and it's better for your chops! Limit the amount of time spent playing repetitious material. Like the scale practice, 25 minutes is a good place to take a break.

Two-octave exercises cover a lot of ground, but we can improvise with smaller pieces of them, too. Remember the smart boxes. We'll plug these chromatics right into more bite-size parcels, but a thought or two before we do: the exercises target one chord tone per exercise, but in application, chromatics can be used on all the chord tones—even in the same line. There was an example of this idea in chapter 4. Remember this?

Chromatic with Multiple Targets

Track 33 - Slow w/Guitar
Track 34 - Slow w/o Guitar
Track 35 - Fast w/Guitar
Track 36 - Fast w/o Guitar

Fig. 9.13. Chromatics with Multiple Targets

Chromatic approaches can be *combined together,* like this:

Combined Approaches in Outline

Track 37 - Slow w/Guitar
Track 38 - Slow w/o Guitar
Track 39 - Fast w/Guitar
Track 40 - Fast w/o Guitar

Fig. 9.14. Combined Approaches in Outline

The first bar of 9.14 combines two of the approaches together. This is a good example of a smart box phrase: less than two octaves register-wise, a clear G–9 outline, and multiple approaches moving side-to-side into the outline. You'll have noticed that I slipped a passing scale tone into this line in bar 2. We're focusing on chromatic approaches here, but always feel free to add content to your lines that helps make them musical.

It's time for you to start writing some lines yourself! You can start by imitating some of the examples I've written here. And the operative word here is *write* (in pencil, with a good eraser)! You'll find that composing lines is a good way of maintaining quality control. What you don't like, you can erase. What you keep becomes part of your vocabulary. Compose lines that contain major, minor, and dominant chord outlines. They can vary in length from one to eight bars or be whatever length you like.

Try recording vamp loops of the chords you're playing over, and play your lines with them. Recycle sections that you like and alter them to fit different chord types. For example, a minor 7 line can become a minor 7♭5 line. When you're pretty successful at that, try moving from one chord to another like this:

Connecting Two Chords

Track 41 - Slow w/Guitar
Track 42 - Slow w/o Guitar
Track 43 - Fast w/Guitar
Track 44 - Fast w/o Guitar

Fig. 9.15. Connecting Two Chords

Example 9.15 contains a few surprises worth examining. Some of the fingerings are a little different, including playing multiple notes on the same string with the same finger. There's an example of what's termed a delayed resolution in the beginning of bar 7 and an example of a line cliché beginning later in that same bar. Analyze and incorporate! You can use these same ingredients in your own lines. Just make sure that you can find the underlying structures that you're building on. With all the stuff that's happening in 9.15, the two basic structures are:

Fig. 9.16. Underlying Chord Structures

You'll notice that I've labeled the preceding chord structure examples as A–7 and C–7, even though both outlines contain the ninth of the chord. Think about them any way you like, but ultimately they are still minor seventh chords. Joe Pass tended to think this way, too. Chords and resultant lines were major, minor, and dominant in nature. Keep things simple!

I hope this helps you to create some boppin' jazz lines and facilitates connecting some chords together! Make sure that you're playing your lines over audio to see how they fit. Now the big challenge! Playing over a jazz tune. The hardest aspect of creating good solo lines is that the chords can be progressing one to the next rapidly. It's one thing to connect chords together in an extended vamp and another thing when the chord duration lasts only two beats! Here are some ideas to help you cope:

- Use chord outlines and partial outlines when the chords are going by quickly.
- Use chromatics, delayed resolution, etc., sparingly.
- Try connecting chord structures on the same string groupings.
- Use space in your lines—a great musical resource!
- Imitate the quality of lines from players you dig (they don't have to be guitarists).

Here's an example of a solo on rhythm changes. Only the solo is included here, with fingerings.

Solo on Rhythm Changes

Track 45 - Slow w/Guitar
Track 46 - Slow w/o Guitar
Track 47 - Fast w/Guitar
Track 48 - Fast w/o Guitar

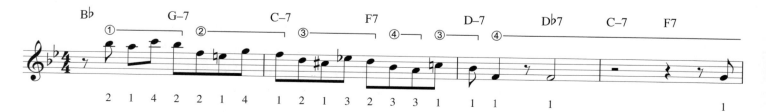

Fig. 9.17. Solo on Rhythm Changes

MAKE IT REAL!

Start some small transcription projects—some Miles Davis or Sonny Rollins, on a tune like "Doxy." Learn the head and the solos. Learn some more bop heads, such as "Anthropology." They contain much the same improv concepts that great solos are made of, plus you're building your repertoire. Write lines!

CHAPTER 10

Soloing: Additional Concepts

IMPROVISING WITH TRIADS: SOME RECYCLING, SOME RETHINKING

Now that we have some foundational ideas about soloing, this is a good point to introduce new concepts based on the previous material. Let's revisit triads. We investigated them briefly in the "Harmony Primer" (chapter 3), and they were used in several examples from "Fingerboard Logistics" (chapter 4) and "Navigating Changes" (chapter 9).

Regardless of type, there are two designations of triad voicings: "close" (sometimes referred to as "tight") and "open" (or "spread"). There are three positions for each type of triad: root position, first inversion, and second inversion, regardless of whether a triad is being designated as "close" or "spread." We'll start by organizing the close position triads.

Triads can be played "across" the neck in string sets of three notes.

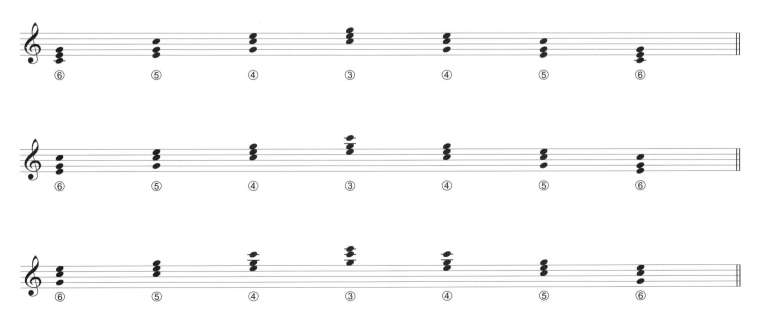

Fig. 10.1. C Major Triads

They can be played laterally on the same string group.

Fig. 10.2. C Major Triads Played Laterally

And, of course, both these previous examples can be played from other string groups and converted to minor, augmented, and diminished, and everything can be played in all keys! A big task, for sure.

Since there are so many options, it helps to focus on one chord type at a time. Major triads can relate to many harmonic situations. You can use close-position major triads to improvise on tunes. Let's try it on this standard jazz progression.

Jazz Progression 3

Track 49 - w/Guitar
Track 50 - w/o Guitar

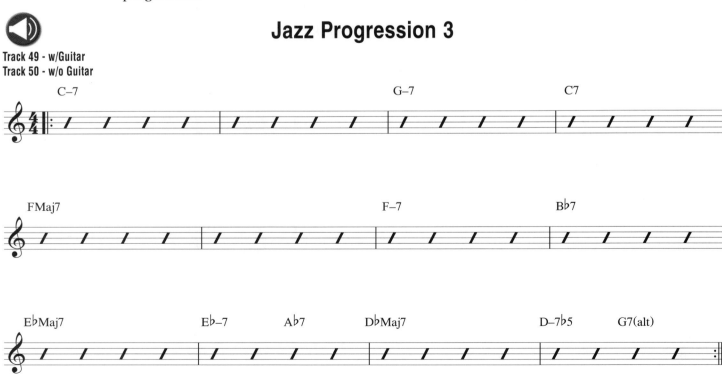

Fig. 10.3. "Solar Flare"

First, assign a major triad to each bar. Obviously, you don't want to play a major triad over a minor chord from the same root. Use the relative major/minor relationship to pick a triad that fits. In this case, play E♭ major over the C–7 chord in the progression. Any time there's a minor chord in the progression, use a major triad built up an interval of a minor third from the minor chord root. Over a major chord, use the major triad from the same root and the same for dominant seventh chords. You can use the major triad in any position. So, step 1 is to choose the triads you want to work with over the chords in the progression. Try a series of triads that are all on the same string group initially. This really helps to link the chords together in a visual way and is effective from a phrasing standpoint, too. Write out the voicings to be clear what you're working with.

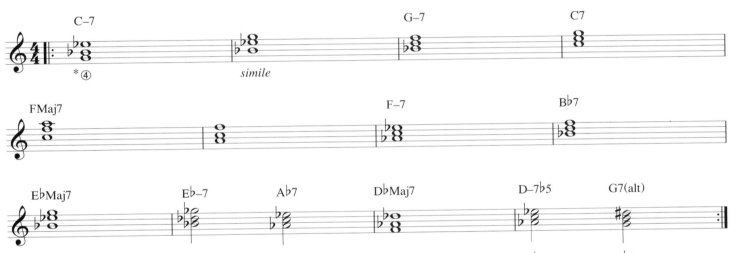

*Note that the lowest note of all these voicings is being played on the fourth string. You can substitute ♭VIMaj7 for D–7♭5.

Fig. 10.4. Triads for "Solar Flare"

Now, we'll start to create a solo study by arpeggiating the chords. We will then arrange the notes of the chord according to different *melodic contours*. Basically, there are four linear combinations in which we can arpeggiate these chords from one to the next, direction-wise:

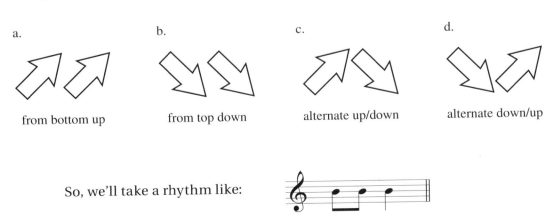

So, we'll take a rhythm like:

Fig. 10.5. Sample Rhythm

Then, we'll use the triads, melodic direction, and the rhythm to create some potential solo content. In these examples, chords lasting a bar in duration repeat the arpeggio twice, and durations lasting two bars get a new chord per bar. Always play the notes of the arpeggio with the same fingers used to play the chord. All four examples use the same voicings and locations from figure 10.4.

Linear Motion Using A

Track 51 - w/Guitar
Track 52 - w/o Guitar

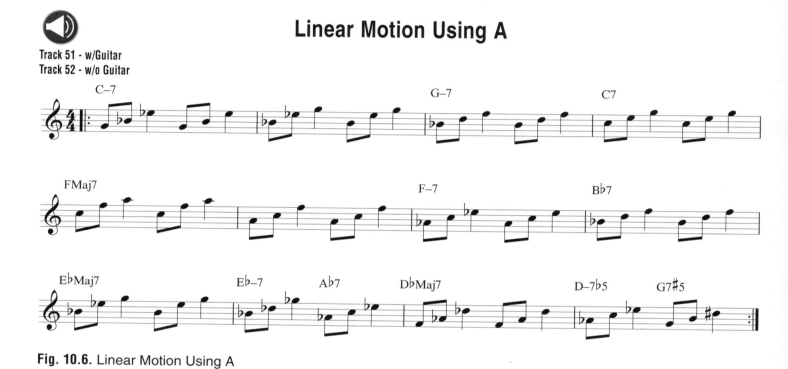

Fig. 10.6. Linear Motion Using A

Linear Motion Using B

Track 53 - w/Guitar
Track 54 - w/o Guitar

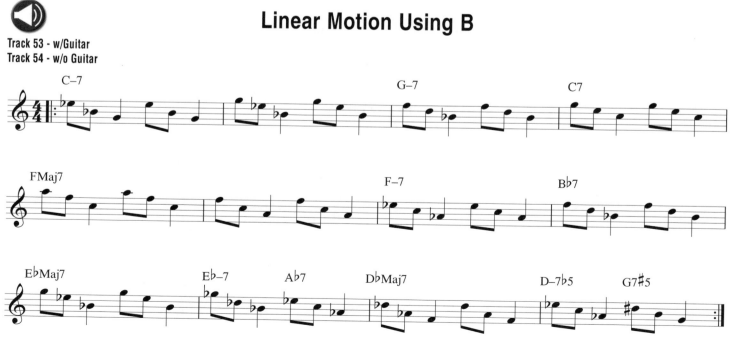

Fig. 10.7. Linear Motion Using B

Remember: the lowest note of all these triad arpeggios is on the fourth string. When making a leap to a new chord voicing, lead with the finger that plays the first note of the arpeggio from the chord shape.

Fig. 10.8. Triad Fingerings on a String Group

Linear Motion Using C

Track 55 - w/Guitar
Track 56 - w/o Guitar

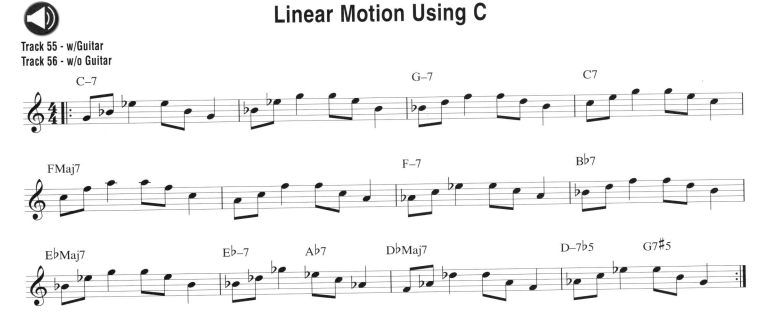

Fig. 10.9. Linear Motion Using C

Linear Motion Using D

Track 57 - w/Guitar
Track 58 - w/o Guitar

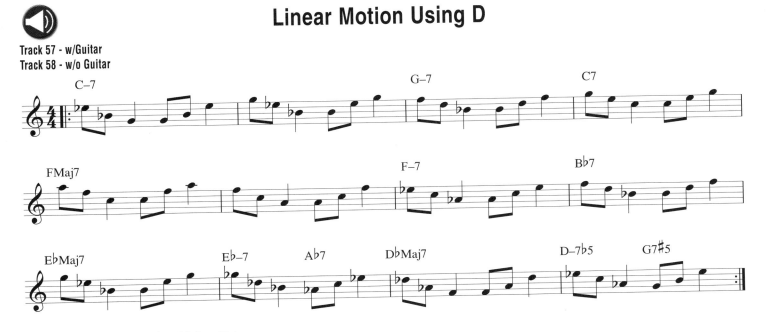

Fig. 10.10. Linear Motion Using D

These preparatory exercises, while pretty bland, are really great practice, and the four types of motion concepts can be applied to all kinds of lines. Ultimately, you should be able to perform these exercises on any progression, even though they are a bit arid, musically. One way to make things hipper is to use some more interesting harmonic detail in the triads you choose. While the goal here is to learn how to use major triads, notice that I slipped an augmented triad over the G7♯5 chord. We could also use an E♭ augmented triad over the first C–7 chord as this is often played C–Maj7. The A♭ major over the D–7♭5 chord is a ♭VI structure in the key. Superimposed on the basic chord, it adds a little spice.

More variants include:

- Use of other rhythms:

Fig. 10.11. Another Rhythm

- Combinations of different rhythms:

Fig. 10.12. Combined Rhythms

- The arpeggio can use repeated notes between chords, such as the E♭ in figure 10.13.

Fig. 10.13. Repeating Notes

- Expand the three string group into a four string group.

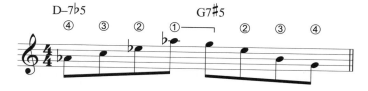

Fig. 10.14. Expanded Strings

Here are some other elements to add variation:

- Use of space.
- Or, leave the space, but if you feel like it, throw (comp) a chord in your lines.
- Use of other content as you like (chromatic or scale approaches, for example).

These last three ideas have great possibilities! Listening to a guitarist like Jim Hall can help you to understand how to insert space around your ideas. Think of the way space around a picture defines that picture more clearly, especially when it's grouped with other pictures. You can see that the analogy works with music, too.

Poppin' a chord in occasionally is a cool way of using space. Use of other content can vary widely. Just don't lose your focus on the content you're trying to control. Add ideas that sound good to you that are "musical" as well as stylistically appropriate.

Here's a one-chorus solo on the changes of "Solar Flare" using the triadic voicings from figure 10.4 and utilizing some of these recent ideas. Fingerings are included to remind you about some of the location concepts we've looked at.

Jazz Progression 3: Solo

Track 59 - w/Guitar
Track 60 - w/o Guitar

Fig. 10.15. "Solar Flare" Solo

A couple of performance notes regarding figure 10.15. You'll notice in a couple of places, like in bar 2, that I use the same finger for all three notes of the triad. Roll the finger between adjacent strings, but also, separate the notes so they don't run together like a chord. There are a couple of unusual fingerings, too. See how you like them.

DIATONIC SCALE TRIADIC HARMONIES: IMPROVISING WITH I IV V STRUCTURES

Another useful triad-based system that I use for improvising is derived from diatonic structures contained in these four primary seven-tone scales.

Fig. 10.16. C Major Diatonic Triads

Fig. 10.17. C Melodic Minor Diatonic Triads

Fig. 10.18. C Harmonic Minor Diatonic Triads

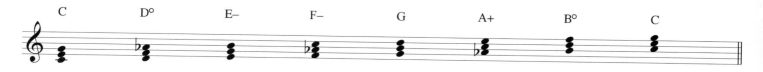

Fig. 10.19. C Harmonic Major Diatonic Triads

There are a gazillion ways you can improvise with these diatonic structures, but I've found a cool way to get some great soloing sounds using just the I, IV, and V triad arpeggios alone. We're "thinking" scales here but breaking them into three-note structures. So, instead of "running" a scale against a chord, we play I, IV, and V triad arpeggios, which contain all the notes of a seven-tone scale to improvise over a diatonically related chord or chords. All of the previous triadic concepts presented apply: string groupings, three- and four-note arpeggio versions, melodic directions, etc. Furthermore, we're applying these I, IV, V "scale packets" over all the diatonic seventh chords, quartal structures, and appropriate tensions related to these four different scales and their offshoot modes.

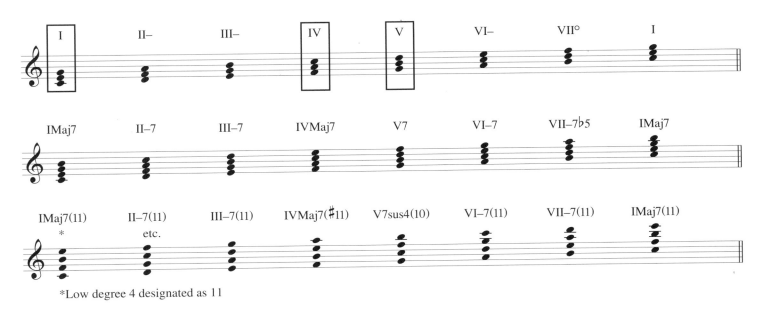

*Low degree 4 designated as 11

Fig.10.20. C Major Diatonic Chord Structures

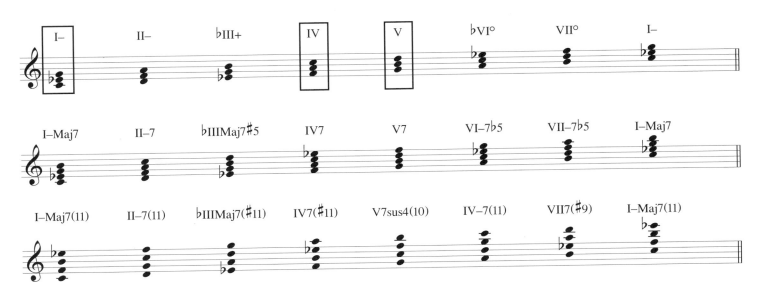

Fig. 10.21. C Melodic Minor Diatonic Chord Structures

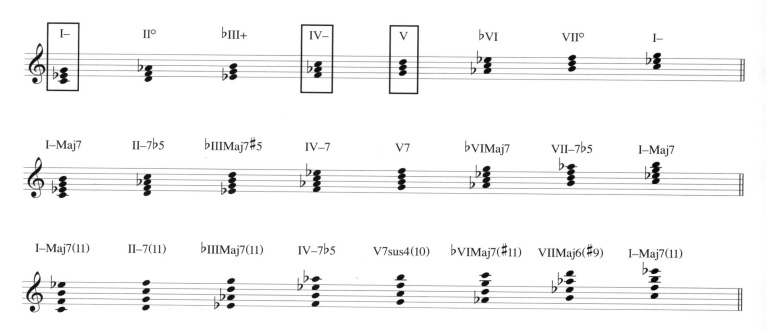

Fig. 10.22. C Harmonic Minor Diatonic Chord Structures

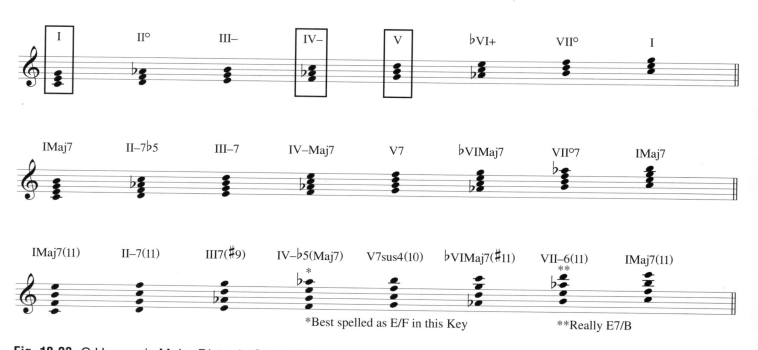

*Best spelled as E/F in this Key   **Really E7/B

Fig. 10.23. C Harmonic Major Diatonic Chord Structures

Let's start with a simple example: vamping on a CMaj7(9) chord. The line shown here is comprised of I, IV, and V triadic structures from a C major scale, in arpeggio form.

C Major I IV V over CMaj7(9)

Track 61 - Slow w/Guitar
Track 62 - Slow w/o Guitar
Track 63 - Fast w/Guitar
Track 64 - Fast w/o Guitar

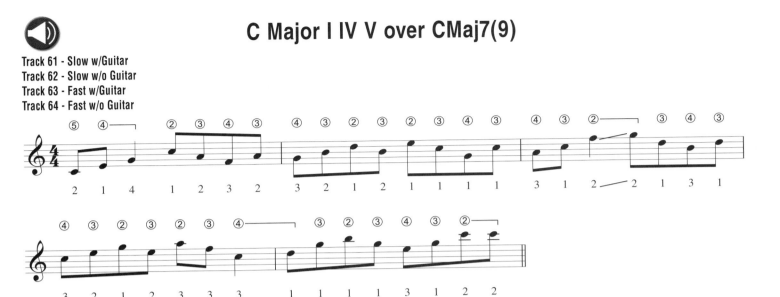

Fig. 10.24. C Major I IV V over CMaj9

You can change the fingerings if you like, but note the string groupings, predominantly strings ②, ③, and ④. This is what contributes to the smooth phrasing. Remember to "separate" the notes so they don't run into each other. You can continue this line in either direction. Play it descending with the same ideas and fingering. Try to play backing chord progressions like D–7 G7 CMaj7, E–7 A7 D–7 G7, and other key-based progressions, while playing the arpeggiated I, IV, V line over these chords. All we're doing here is playing the scale in "parcels" of three notes. This helps the melodic quality of the line by getting some intervallic space between the notes and adds the melody-building tool of sequence at the same time.

The I IV V concept will work over all the diatonic chords listed above in the four "master" scales. You just need to change the basic triad structure to fit the scale. For instance, look at the harmonic major scale. The scale uses a ♭6, which now makes the triads I, IV–, V. Alter the line in figure 10.24 to change the IV chord to minor, and try it over an E7(♯9) chord vamp (the third structure of quartalized harmonic major). You might come up with something like figure 10.25.

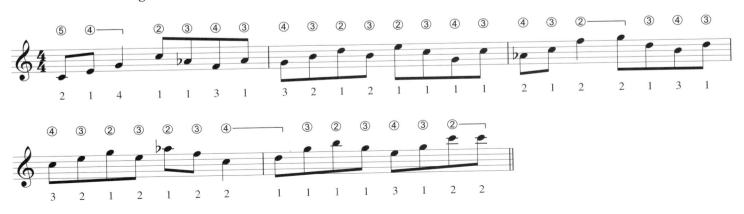

Fig. 10.25. C Harmonic Major I IV V over E7(♯9)

If this feels a little strange initially, try mixing in some of these I, IV, V concepts in with some lines you already play. Try transposing them to other chord roots, and find the corresponding transposed scale that relates diatonically, i.e., D7(#9) could relate to B♭ harmonic major. Your musical taste combined with experimentation, writing, and listening will yield some interesting applications of this concept. Try it with spread triads, too. Definitely use backing tracks (vamps, II Vs, etc.) to "ground" your results in reality. There is a relationship between these scales and every chord under the sun!

Another Idea: Scale Fragments/Patterns

One way to rethink using scales for improvising is to use portions (or a fragment) of the scale over chord changes. Often, a fragment, usually known as a "pattern"—like 1, 2, 3, 5—can be common to several scales and chords. For instance, this 1, 2, 3, 5 pattern is common to Ionian, Lydian, and Mixolydian, making it usable over major and dominant seventh chords.

A scale pattern can be modified, for instance, by changing one or more of the tones or by relating to the scale degrees of another scale. The pattern 1, 2, 3, 5 could be modified to 1, 2, ♭3, 5 and related to minor chords and melodic, harmonic, and natural-minor scales. A four-eighth-note pattern applied to a progression, such as these changes used in tunes such as "Giant Steps" might look like this:

Jazz Progression 4

Track 65 - Slow w/Guitar
Track 66 - Slow w/o Guitar
Track 67 - Fast w/Guitar
Track 68 - Fast w/o Guitar

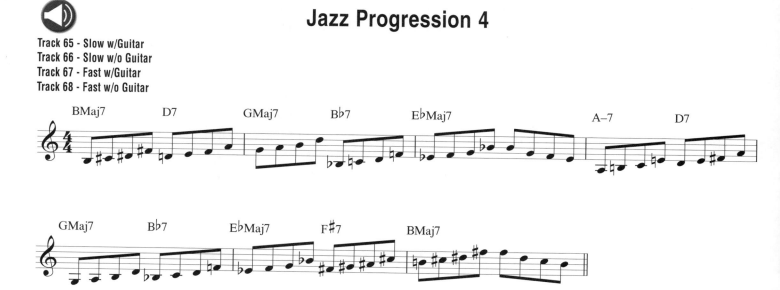

Fig. 10.26. Pattern 1, 2, 3, 5 on "Giant Steps" Changes

Notice that on the major seventh chords that last for an entire bar, the pattern has been repeated but in reverse, using line motion C. Apply line motion C to the progression, and we get the variation with the second chord in each bar played retrograde (backwards).

Fig. 10.27. Pattern 1, 2, 3, 5 Using Line Motion

The patterns would look like this, combining line motion D for one bar, then C for a bar.

Fig. 10.28. Pattern 1, 2, 3, 5 Using Line Motion D and C

As you can see, there is a lot of possible variation here! And what makes things really exciting is to analyze John Coltrane's solo on "Giant Steps." There are not only scale patterns but chord arpeggios, as well. Some of the chord arpeggios are triadic, some are seventh chords with tensions. Coltrane frequently played combinations of scale patterns and chord outlines in couplets in his solos. The "Giant Steps" progression is based on a major chord moving to a dominant seventh chord up a minor third or, enharmonically, an augmented second (a "giant step").

Fig. 10.29. Steps Progression

Lines made from the two chords can be organized into "couplets." Check out Coltrane's solo, and list the patterns, then combine some of the patterns together, like this couplet.

Fig. 10.30. Pattern Couplet

These two patterns could be analyzed as 1, 2, 3, 5 and 9, ♭7, 6, 5. You can plug them into an improvisation on a progression such as the one used in "Giant Steps," and transpose the couplet as needed.

Fig. 10.31. Transposing a Couplet

The progression used in "Giant Steps" is a fascinating one and a real challenge to play over. What we want to take from it right now is an understanding of how to combine scales and chord outlines that we can harness for our own solos. This couplet and pattern concept also works well on any two changes per bar scenario similar to this II V progression.

Fig. 10.32. Patterns and Couplets on II V Progression

We could mix some of these ideas to combine with previous concepts in the "Solar Flare" solo (figure 10.15).

Jazz Progression 3 Triads/Patterns

Track 69 - w/Guitar
Track 70 - w/o Guitar

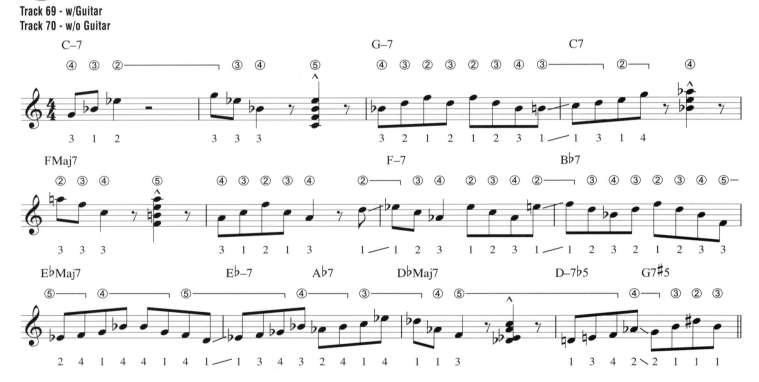

Fig. 10.33. Combining Triads with Patterns on "Solar Flare"

Notice that a couple of fingerings have been changed to incorporate some of the patterns and their connection. This is still pretty basic stuff, but you're making the changes! This is a good way to practice your solo writing ideas. Add on to something you've already written, and make a variation. Instead of using completely new ideas each time, you'll make new solos based on material that you've got under control. Is this spontaneous improvisation? No, but it's the craft work that leads us in the right direction. The ingredients need to be organized, fingered, and practiced before any of these concepts will become intuitive in their usage.

PENTATONIC SCALES

The study of pentatonic scales in jazz improvisation is a long-term undertaking. As "practical jazz guitarists," we need to look at some ideas we can use now. Why look at pentatonics? Many of us start out playing rock music where pentatonic scale usage is widespread. Often, when we start playing jazz, we tend to turn our backs on the past, trying to move on to new territory, and we may forget to use a tool that we already have together playing-wise.

Pentatonics were/are used by supreme artists like Coltrane, McCoy Tyner, Herbie Hancock, and just about any great guitarist you can mention. We just need to reexamine how and where we might use it to our advantage. This basic minor seventh pentatonic scale is most often the first thing a guitarist learns how to play. It's also very close in nature to a minor seventh-chord arpeggio.

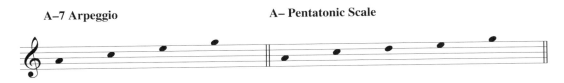

Fig. 10.34. A–7 Arpeggio and A Minor-Pentatonic Scale

What I like about pentatonic scales is that they're a connection between scales and chord outlines. Using all triads or seventh chord outlines tends to yield a line that moves mainly by leaps. This can add a "jagged" quality to a line, while a scale line can be too "smooth." Too much of either gets predictable. The pentatonic scale is a combination of leaps and stepwise motion, like other scales, but smaller and easier to manipulate yet still containing some leap motion—a contrast. This balance is a good thing for creating interesting line contour.

So, what are pentatonic scales and how can we make use of them? The root "penta" is a Greek root for five, so the pentatonic scale is comprised of five notes. Interestingly, each note of the scale can form its own "mode" of the scale. The minor-seventh pentatonic that we're all familiar with is actually an offshoot of this major-sixth scale.

Fig. 10.35. C Major Sixth Pentatonic Scale

In jazz, the pentatonic scale is frequently used in sequence. Here's how to practice them in sequence. (We'll use the A–7 pentatonic scale we're already familiar with, as an example.)

First, take the scale and stack all the notes from the scale on each scale tone.

Fig. 10.36. Pentatonic Scale Stacked

Now, play the five notes stacked on each scale degree as a single-line quintuplet.

Fig. 10.37. Pentatonic Sequence on A Minor

Try it down an octave, too.

Fig. 10.38. Pentatonic Sequence on A Minor 8vb

Count the bottom note of each scale stack as one and the highest note as five. The sequences we just created are 1, 2, 3, 4, 5. If we changed the numbers to 1, 2, 3, 5, 4, the sequence would look like this.

Fig. 10.39. Pentatonic Sequence on A Minor 8vb: 1, 2, 3, 5, 4

It would be the same notes if you play in the higher octave too, just 8va. Try all these permutations with this minor-pentatonic scale:

1, 2, 3, 4, 5   1, 2, 3, 5, 4   1, 2, 4, 3, 5   1, 2, 4, 5, 3   1, 2, 5, 3, 4   1, 2, 5, 4, 3

This is just a start! These sequences can be done in rhythmic units other than five-note groups, too. This next one is in groups of four, and they can also reverse direction while descending, like in this example.

Fig. 10.40. Pentatonic Sequence on A Minor: Four Note Groups

If we numbered the previous group 1, 2, 3, 4, we could make permutations here as well. This would be 1, 2, 4, 3, but there are many more.

Fig. 10.41. Pentatonic Sequence on A Minor: 1, 2, 4, 3

Try writing these sequences out, if you need to, but make sure you learn to play them. Sequences teach your hands how to hear on the fingerboard, and they are great improv material, as well. Using or completing a sequence while improvising conveys a thought that is completed. It's similar to finishing a sentence while speaking.

While we've been looking at an A minor-pentatonic scale and some sequences, the beauty of this particular scale is its relationship to many chords for improvising—not just A minor. Initially, we tend to think about improvising with content from a scale over a chord with the same root. The pitch collection of the five notes in this scale relate to many different harmonies—some basic, some a little more advanced. Try improvising melodies with this A minor-pentatonic scale and its sequences over these chords:

Chord	Minor Pentatonic from
A–7	(from R)
D–7	(from 5)
CMaj7	(from 6)
FMaj7	(from 3)
B♭Maj7	(from 7)
D9	(from 5)
F♯7(alt)	(from ♭3)
A♭7(alt)	(from ♭2)

This is just a beginning list. Record the chord changes, and try running some sequences over the basic chords on the list. Try transposing the scale and sequences to other chords. Select one of the above chords, then pick a different root, and apply the scale relationship as listed above. For instance, play G7(alt) and try a B♭ minor pentatonic or an A♭ minor pentatonic. Make notes of what you like. When working on improvising over a tune, try writing the relationships over the basic changes, like this:

Fig. 10.42. Targeting Changes with Pentatonic Scales

Jot down a few lines, and make some music out of these ideas. Here are three vamps where the same scale is moving parallel on the fingerboard. Note the frequency of fourth intervals in the following lines.

Swing: Pentatonic Example A

Track 71 - w/Guitar
Track 72 - w/o Guitar

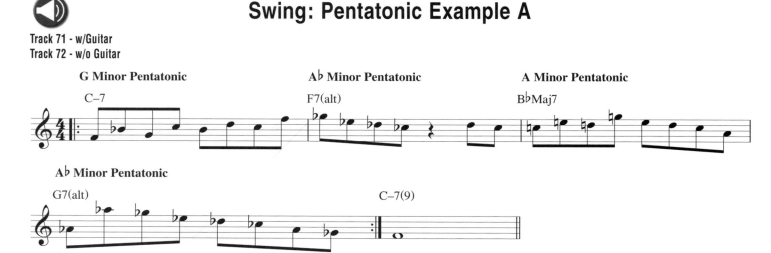

Fig. 10.43. Moving Pentatonic Vamp A: Swing

Latin: Pentatonic Example B

Track 73 - w/Guitar
Track 74 - w/o Guitar

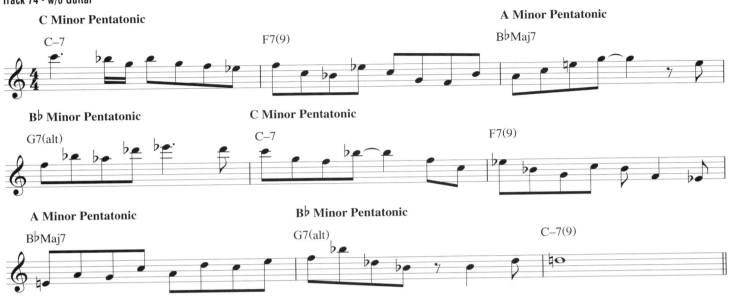

Fig. 10.44. Moving Pentatonic Vamp B: Latin

Swing: Pentatonic Example C

Track 75 - w/Guitar
Track 76 - w/o Guitar

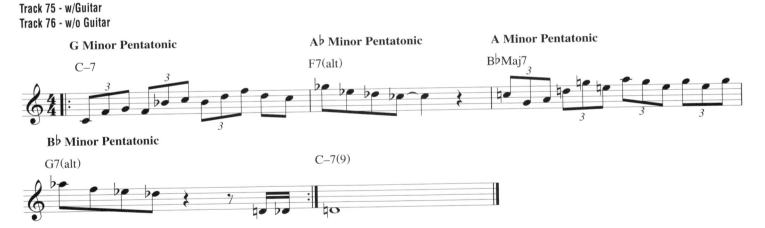

Fig. 10.45. Moving Pentatonic Vamp C: Swing

MAKE IT REAL!

There are a lot of ideas to work with in this chapter. Try to organize and write some of these ideas into a jazz tune improvisation. Target places in tunes where you want to try something specific. Not all of the ideas need to be used together. Most important of all, keep listening to the great ones to get a sense of what's appropriate, stylistically.

CHAPTER 11

Ear Training

Ear training is the most important aspect of any guitarist's training. Traditional music training in Europe usually started with a year of sight-singing before a student attempted to learn an instrument. Suzuki and other methodologies start with singing and movement exercises that are preparatory to or concurrent with instrumental study. But, most guitarists usually start out learning on their own instrument first. With the media explosion of how-to books and YouTube videos, along with downloadable lessons, today's guitarist has access to more information than ever before, and, guitar in hand, we learn.

It's natural for guitar players to gravitate to playing the instrument before training the ear, and this book is not dedicated to ear training. There are many resources available for ear training, available in every medium. But, think about it: ear training is the foundation for playing in tune and identifying what's happening around us—like knowing where we are in a song form, and so on. It also helps us to identify musical devices for improvising, and to create and react to harmony, rhythm, and what our fellow performers are playing. So, what could be more important than ear training?

TUNING YOUR GUITAR: MICRO EAR TRAINING

Let's start at the beginning: being able to tune your guitar and recognizing gradations of sharp and flat.

Tuning your guitar is a prerequisite for successful playing. But you would be surprised how many players can't tune their guitars accurately without an electronic tuner. Tuning is almost a forgotten art. Electronic tuners *are* useful when you're trying to tune your guitar in a noisy environment. Unfortunately, we've become so dependent on them that many of us have lost the ability to tune without one. This kind of skill is what I call "micro" ear training. To become a better musician and a superlative guitarist, it's crucial to develop this skill. It is also an important component of setting up and "tempering" intonation on a guitar.

There are several methods that guitarists use to tune their guitars, such as matching unisons on the fifth fret with open strings, matching harmonics between the fifth and seventh frets, and more. One of the best methods I've found can be attributed to guitarist Johnny Smith. Legend has it that Johnny used this method not only to tune his own guitar but to test and set the intonation on a batch of the Gibson Johnny Smith model guitars before they were shipped from the factory. That's professional commitment! Here's his method:

1. Tune the first string to your reference note.
2. Match the open E string to the fretted E on the B string at the fifth fret.
3. Match the fretted E on the G string at the ninth fret to the open E string.
4. Match the fretted B on the D string at the ninth fret to the open B string.
5. Match the fretted G on the A string at the tenth fret to the open G string.
6. Match the fretted D on the low E string at the tenth fret to the open D string.

Here's another variation I like to tune with which uses harmonics with fretted notes.

1. Tune the first string to your reference note.
2. Play the B harmonic on the second string at the twelfth fret, and match this pitch to the fretted B on the first string, seventh fret.
3. Play the G harmonic on the third string, twelfth fret, and match it to the fretted G on the first string, third fret.
4. Play the D harmonic on the fourth string, twelfth fret, and match it to the fretted D on the second string, third fret.
5. Play the A harmonic on the fifth string, twelfth fret, and match it to the fretted A on the third string, second fret.
6. Lastly, play the E harmonic on the twelfth fret, and match it to the fretted E on the fourth string, second fret.

The trick here is to let the harmonic note sustain as you compare the fretted note, as in Johnny Smith's method. You'll notice that the two notes will "beat" against one another until you get the fretted note in tune with the harmonics or an open string. If you haven't done this before, it can take a little time to get the hang of it. It's easier to think of the notes as visually represented by a waveform, which you can "draw" with your hand in the air. When the two notes are tuned, the waveform will be a "flat" wave (line) with no beating. You'll gain the sense of when the notes are sharp or flat with some practice. Try "drawing" the out of tune wave with your hand for a visual reference. Getting back to the guitar, once you have any note in either sequence tuned, *do not* go back and tweak the previously tuned pitch!

Guitar Intonation

Once you have completed the entire string-tuning sequence, if your guitar is not in tune, you probably have some intonation issues. One cause of faulty intonation is old strings. Old strings, especially the trebles, go flat and need to be changed regularly. If you've changed strings and the guitar still won't tune, then chances are your bridge needs intonation tweaking.

Most people are afraid to mess around with this job and take it to a "pro" to be done, which is fine. But, there will be times when a guitar tech is not available. Once you can hear when notes are sharp or flat, you can try intoning the guitar yourself. There are basically two kinds of bridges: fixed wood (or metal), usually a carved piece of wood, and "Tune-o-matic," with individually adjustable saddles. On the fixed variety, the best method is to set the middle of the bridge at the correct string length from the nut, then shift the treble or bass sides of the bridge for the truest intonation. Usually, you can get a "visual" fix on this placement by observing the bridge feet in relation to the "F" holes. A word of caution: with this kind of bridge, be careful not to dig your fingernails into the top of the guitar as you position the bridge. Many jazz guitars have a spruce top that dents easily!

A few examples of typical well-known guitar string lengths are:

25.5" scale L5, Super 400, Stratocaster, Telecaster

25", 25.1", 25.4" scale Gibson Johnny Smith, Benedetto guitars, Borys Guitar

24.75" Les Paul, SG, 175, ES 335, ES 345, ES 355

23.5" (short scale) Gibson Byrdland, ES 350T

To measure a guitar's scale length, use a measuring tape to measure from the nut to the middle of the bridge, roughly around the space between the D and G strings. Once you have the bridge in the ballpark, or if you have a fixed bridge, the routine is the same: Start by playing the octave harmonic at the twelfth fret, then compare the fretted note at the same location. If the fretted note is sharp, move the saddle or the bridge away from the nut (making the string length longer). If the note is flat, do the opposite and move the saddle/bridge closer toward the nut (making the string length shorter). I'm talking about really small adjustments here! This method will do for a quick fix, but for a pro's ear, go on to compare the harmonic at the nineteenth fret along with the fretted note on the same fret, and use the same procedure on each string. You may find with a fixed bridge that some "concessions" have to be made to "temper" your guitar, but end by matching the harmonic and the fretted note at the nineteenth fret on both the high and low E strings.

Some guitars with "tune-o-matic" bridges have issues, too. The Gibson ES 335 with its 24.75 scale frequently has a sharp G string, which sometimes can be cured by reversing the saddle and getting a little more string length. Each guitar has its little quirks, but some experimentation and experience helps. You *can* do it yourself!

Once you tune your ear into hearing these smaller pitch increments, you'll realize just how important this kind of hearing is. Intonation in ensemble playing is crucial! And there's nothing so frustrating as recording an inspired solo, only to discover upon playback that it's way out of tune. That's why great producers make the big bucks: Because they can hear this! Nowadays, pro engineers, and even players with project studios, can "auto-tune" an out-of-tune track to an extent, but good intonation and well set-up instruments are the mark of a pro guitarist. Not to mention that if you're paying big money to record, you're better off going for good takes rather than having an engineer fix faulty parts electronically!

EAR TRAINING EXERCISES

Now that we've looked at "micro tuning," let's go on to some standard ear training technique. The method described here was used by the great jazz pedagogue, Charlie Banacos, with all his students. You can practice it on guitar or with a piano and a pencil. The pencil needs a good eraser on it, as you will see!

On piano, play a I IV V I cadence in the key of C. (Even a guitarist can easily do this on a piano by "blocking" the three-note chords on the piano or keyboard.)

Make sure that you can sing the note C after playing the cadence for your ears' reference. (Also, pitch matching is an important skill and is tested for in school auditions.)

Turn your back on the piano after playing the cadence and strike a note with the pencil, eraser-side down! Without trying to think too much, name the note. After you decide, always check to make sure you've got the right note! Avoid singing up or down to the key's tonic and singing interval fragments from songs like "Here Comes the Bride," or "Twinkle, Twinkle Little Star." The idea is to identify the note without any intermediary step.

If you find this difficult, try practicing by playing the cadence, then limiting your choices visually to the tonic, then the fifth, then the thirds, sevenths, seconds, fourths, sixths, then all the non-diatonic notes to C major. Start with an area of the piano that is in your vocal range; sing and match all of the pitches you play. Then, move the pencil over the entire range of the piano, low and high, to test yourself, and do the procedure rapidly.

As for naming the pitches, feel free to just say a scale or note degree like "5" or "♭6," or a note name like "G" or "A♭." If you already do solfege, feel free to use the Do, Re, Mi syllables. Start by doing the procedure only in C, as this has certain benefits. Later you can do the cadence in any key, and relate the notes to that key. Obviously, all of this can also be done on the guitar as well; just skip the pencil.

This may take a while to get together, but keep at it. This is an important step in training your ear, particularly because identifying the "colors" relative to a tonal center has so many benefits for us in all musical situations. For instance, you'll learn to hear the difference between major and minor, whether a fifth is raised or lowered, and what tensions are being added to a chord type.

Once you can do one-note ear training flawlessly, it's time to do two notes. It's built on the same principal as one-note ear training, but has an added twist.

Play the I IV V I cadence in C, and sing and hold the note C while you strike two random notes on the keyboard.

Identify the quality of the C you're singing relative to a key inferred by the two notes you played. For instance, the C might sound like "3" or "♭5" of a key. Identify the key, and then identify the two pitches you played relative to that key.

This method continues up to eleven notes, where you have to identify the one note that isn't being played. Obviously the piano is the instrument of choice here, to get that many notes, though you can still apply multiple notes on the guitar, up to a reasonable point. I recommend that you don't add additional notes until you can flawlessly hear each level: two notes, then three notes, etc. Recording the procedure at each level of notes is a good idea, too. Record, say, twenty-five examples of the cadence and three notes, and then listen to and identify them a couple of days later.

Along with the ear training examples above, I recommend that you try to sing what you play. For those planning to audition at music schools, be aware that you will be expected to match pitch and sing/playback on your instrument as a part of an audition. (See the appendix for ear training exercises you can use with the CD.) Singing, whether it's a solo, roots of a chord progression, or in whatever form, helps us internalize music. So, make singing and ear training a part of your daily routine.

MAKE IT REAL!

Eventually, having mastered some of the material here, consider joining your school choir, or taking an online solfege/ear training course to improve your singing/musicianship skills. This chapter will get you started, but many students do ear training best in a structured, class setting, with regular homework, and teacher feedback.

CHAPTER 12

Reading

WHY GUITARISTS HAVE TROUBLE READING

What is it about sight-reading that makes us guitarists tremble in our boots? Having done clinics, led ensembles, and given countless finals and auditions the world over, I've heard "my reading's terrible!" and "dude, my reading sucks!" countless times and in many languages. Guitar players are legendary for being bad sight-readers. So, why do guitarists have so much more trouble reading than other instrumentalists?

There are several reasons. First off, most guitarists don't start playing until their teen years. Most string, brass, and woodwind players begin their instrumental lessons during elementary school, and the lessons are usually reading-oriented. They have to be, because the schools need these kids to participate in ensembles like concert band, wind ensemble, orchestra, etc. Those ensembles play written music, so to participate, you have to read. Right there, students who have "learned" their axe via reading have several years of reading on their instrument and playing in reading situations under their belts by the time they're teenagers.

Another issue with guitarists and sight-reading is that many of us learn by copying recordings of our favorite players. Personally, I consider this to be an important aspect of any guitarist's musical training. There are those who frown upon transcribing as leading to a loss of originality and not paying attention to "one's inner voice," etc., but the fact is that playing along with transcriptions forces us to make decisions about fingering and connectivity—important formative concepts for guitarists. There's also a wealth of nuance one gains from playing along with recordings, not to mention the development of "touch." What does this have to do with sight-reading? The answer is that most of us don't notate our transcriptions. This is great for the ear, but bad from the perspective of developing reading skills.

Furthermore, many guitarists document their transcriptions in "tab." Tablature is good for us guitarists, but undecipherable to other musicians who don't play guitar. So as useful as tab is, it also isolates us from other intru-mentalists who use traditional notation as a means of conveying musical ideas. Once again, we're putting off the issue of learning to read.

Finally, another reason why guitarists have difficulty sight-reading is the issue of note duplication. The guitar, with its six strings and tuning in fourths, has many duplicated notes all over the fingerboard. Many instruments, such as the piano, have only one location for a particular note, say middle C. That middle C might be played with any finger in the course of a piece, but will always remain at that one location on the keyboard. Horn players have valve or key fingerings that correspond to a note. Outside of the occasional "false fingering" or "extended technique," they pretty much hit a note with one or sometimes two valve/key fingerings. Not so on the guitar! We have so many options for where to locate/play a note, that by the time we've made up our minds where to play it, the band is on the next piece! There is definitely a "lag" time associated with this location issue. We'll come back to this in a while.

Now that we've identified some of the causes of guitarists tending to be weak readers, let's explore some ways we can improve our reading.

First, you have to know why you're having difficulty. Try reading this excerpt from one of my tunes, "The Bonga."

Fig. 12.1. "The Bonga" Excerpt

It's a fairly challenging excerpt. How did you do? Did you play it in time? Did you "nail it" on the first try? If not, let's explore a routine to improve your reading.

Reading is equal parts of experience, performance, ear training, and know-how. But initially, you need to know which elements to concentrate on to improve.

I've found it helpful to break down the reading process into three areas of study.

Step 1 is training your eye to decipher each pitch on the staff, translating it into a letter name. Read off the names of this next example as fast as you can say the letter name A, B♭, C♯, etc.

Fig. 12.2. Medium Register; Most Notes in the Scale

How did you do? If you were pretty fast rattlin' off the pitch names, try this low register example.

Fig. 12.3. Lower Register

Once again, if you did pretty well with the last example, continue with this next high register example.

Fig. 12.4. Higher Register

Many students will do fairly well naming the pitches in the first example (medium register), get a little slower on the low register, and then become downright "turtle-like" when it comes to the last high-register one. The cognitive ability to recognize any pitch in any register on the staff is an essential ingredient to becoming a better sight-reader. If you find yourself fumbling for names, "A... flat... B... C..., no D♯," then you need to train your eye to recognize the pitches faster. And since it's common for people to have more trouble with low and high registers, I suggest you write out three pages of notes (no rhythm, just whole notes, like the preceding examples) that are completely random and skipping around in medium, low, and high registers, and then practice training your eye until you get fast at naming the pitches.

Another "eye-training" exercise is to follow a score or part while listening to a recording. Getting the sense of the duration of each measure of music in time, and following the bars from system to system, trains the eye how to jump distances and get a sense of the spatial layout of the music, as it relates to time.

Step 2 involves rhythm. Often, this is many students' "weakest link" that causes them to be poor readers on guitar. If your sense of rhythm in time is weak, you will have great difficulty reading in time. Typically, a guitarist with poor rhythm recognition gets behind in the piece, loses the sense of time, then "crashes and burns." This is another basic "musicianship skills" issue that, along with the note recognition, can be practiced without the guitar in hand. In fact, you're better off not bringing the issues of location and guitar technique into the process at this point! So, to practice rhythm recognition, put down the guitar, and start conducting! Conducting? YEAH, conducting!

Conducting scares some people, but I find that it's the best way of instilling a steady sense of meter while practicing rhythms. The right hand (which conducts the beat patterns) takes on an almost "autopilot" state after some practice. When you can conduct and sing rhythms "against" the beat pattern (while keeping things steady) accurately, this aspect of "musicianship skills" will transfer to your guitar sight-reading. There are several good books to practice with that specifically target rhythm studies. Robert Starer's book *Rhythmic Training* (Alfred Publishing, 1999) is an excellent one to start with. Also try Steve Prosser's book, *Essential Ear Training* (Berklee Press, 2000) for conducting patterns and other ear training strategies. And, of course, you can practice conducting and singing rhythms with any piece of written music, from jazz tunes in the *Real Book* to excerpts from a Beethoven symphony. One word of caution: start with simple material, master it, then gradually work on harder pieces.

When you have pretty good control of steps 1 and 2, it's time to start thinking about organizational and fingering concepts on the guitar. Traditionally, most guitar methods start at the bottom of the fingerboard with open strings and then work gradually higher on the neck in positions. It makes sense to limit the range of activity like this; you can't learn it all at once. However, playing using this approach tends to compromise the quality of phrasing, especially with jazz music. I've seen students trying to read a jazz guitar transcription in position, and they don't get very good results. An antidote can be found by studying the chapter, "Scales and Modes." That chapter focuses on playing scales, which contain many arpeggio fingerings and chord grips within the boundaries of the scale fingering. The scales are presented in one-, two-, and three-octave versions, as well as different orientations and locations. This can help you start thinking about this third aspect of reading: execution/location.

Finding the ideal location to play is similar to improvising. When we improvise, though there may be moments of pure spontaneity, many of our ideas come from craftwork. These are ideas that have been worked out and practiced enough to be "spontaneously rearranged" with other ideas on the fly, in an interactive way. The association with reading is that when we read, we're analyzing/listening for content that suggests location. Of course, this can vary widely with the sophistication of the musical content that we're reading.

Let's look at an example of how to determine where to play something. This fragment of "Deck the Halls" is comprised of notes completely diatonic to C major.

Options where it could be played include:

- in "open" position, utilizing open strings

- in many movable positions related to C major scales

- starting on the sixth, fifth, or fourth strings, and using adjacent strings

- completely on one string at a time, starting on the sixth or fifth strings

Fig. 12.5. Fragment of "Deck the Halls"

Next, consider a more difficult example: another fragment of "The Bonga." It contains elements of pentatonic scales, as well as polychordal fragments of triadic and quintal harmony. Because its register is limited to notes mainly in the staff, it is playable in a few places, but my choices for fingering would be dictated by the pentatonic and arpeggio content. Can you identify these elements?

Fig. 12.6. "The Bonga" Fragment 2

You can see that, simple or difficult, there is usually more than one location to play the music in. Choices as to where to play an idea become part habit, style, and listening to what the music dictates. Start by analyzing the music you're trying to read for content. Some line passages will be scalar and some made of arpeggio content. There are also passing notes that will be chromatic or delayed resolutions, etc. Try to "see" the basic content to find a fingering from something you know, such as a scale fragment or a major triad arpeggio form.

Reading Etude 1

Analyze and play this etude, and try to find fingerings related to the given harmonies. Remember, there isn't just one way to do it, so experiment!

Fig. 12.7. Reading Etude 1

You may notice at this point that some of these reading examples have been challenging. These are not easy. The "Bonga" fragments are "pro" level, and the etude would be college level—somewhere around fourth semester. Only "Deck the Halls" is considered simple level.

Get a sense of what level you're at, and try to find similar material that is challenging and interesting, but not so difficult that you can't get through it. You're much better off starting at a level that you can play musically without too many mistakes. This builds confidence, which is an important ingredient for developing reading skills. There are tons of materials available for you to practice reading, such as *Reading Studies for Guitar* and *Advanced Reading Studies for Guitar*, by William Leavitt (Berklee Press). Also look for books of excerpts, duets, etc. of classical music.

Regardless of your level, you can still apply the three areas of focus (along with a little common sense) and really improve your reading. Here are some recaps and thoughts on how to proceed.

- Choose material that is appropriate to your current level of reading skill. There are many sources to procure material from. Try some "classical" excerpt books, or books of duets (practice with a friend). Books come in an assortment of levels and are available through many famous publishing houses. Some books might be written for flute, clarinet, etc. but will work fine for guitar, as long as you don't get into transposition issues when playing with non-concert instruments.

- Before you actually try the piece, go through the three steps:

  1. Identify the notes by "eye," and practice following the notes in time, with a metronome, from system to system.

  2. Practice the rhythms by conducting and singing just the rhythms through the piece.

  3. Analyze the piece for content and determine where to locate/play what you find. Look for scale fragments and arpeggio/chord shapes. Understand the function of notes like chromatics, etc., and how they relate to the piece's overall content. At that point, proceed to try the piece. Use a metronome to mark your progress. Start at a slow tempo, then increase the speed as you get comfortable with the music. Try singing along with the music, to internalize it. There's a strong connection between pitch recall and singing.

- Differentiate between reading and sight-reading. Sight-reading is a piece that you read with no preparation, on the spot. Try to do some of this every day. The material should be simple at first, then increasing in difficulty as your skills improve. This will help you determine how quickly you're implementing the three factors above. Look for pieces with some long-duration notes, simple rhythms, and easy-to-analyze content. Figure 12.8 is an example of basic material, like what you might start out practicing. Before you play it, take twenty seconds to scan it for detail.

Fig. 12.8. Easy Reading Example

Reading "The Bonga" cold will be *really* difficult. Try it, though. Go through each system, and try reading it in smaller chunks, say, four bars at a time. Use a metronome to keep yourself honest. Start slowly then speed up the tempo. This would be an example of a piece you would work up gradually while reading, but not on the spot.

The Bonga

Mark White

Fig. 12.9. "The Bonga" (Complete Lead Sheet)

MAKE IT REAL!

- Find new materials to read.

- Get together with a friend and read.

- Read every day!

CHAPTER 13

Auditioning for Schools and Scholarships

Auditioning for a music school is not always as cut-and-dried as it sounds. Whether you're auditioning for a summer program, admission to a music school, or to garner scholarship monies, it's really important to understand what will help you achieve a successful outcome. I have done literally hundreds of auditions for the Berklee College of Music in Boston and at many of their BIN (Berklee International Network) schools across the globe. I can tell you from experience that many young musicians don't really know specifics of the process that might have a significant impact on their education and careers. Let's look at some details to help you do well in your auditions and quest for scholarship funding.

NUMBER ONE RULE: COME PREPARED!

Sounds obvious, right? Actually, many students show up at auditions without knowing what they're expected to play at the audition. My suggestion here is to carefully research the specific requirements for each particular school, which can vary widely. For instance, many music schools require specific repertoire for an audition. This is very common in "classical" conservatories and orchestral auditions, which detail specific pieces or choices from a "period," such as a piece by J.S. Bach from the baroque period, or by Fernando Sor from the classical period, or a modern work by Villa Lobos. Music schools that offer contemporary and jazz music programs often require specific jazz pieces by Charlie Parker or composers from the bop era. So, do your research before you audition!

Check out a school's website or request written information via mail to find out what you need to prepare. Berklee, in particular, has extensive web-based information about the audition procedures and provides downloadable lead sheets and play-along recordings to help in the preparation.

IF YOU CAN, CHOOSE PIECES THAT REPRESENT THE "REAL YOU," MUSICALLY.

One doesn't always get a free hand in the choice of audition material. But some schools (like Berklee) feature a wide array of majors and musical genres. You don't necessarily have to play a "jazz" piece at your audition because an institution is well-known for its jazz program—unless you like to play jazz. You're really better off playing what's natural for you to play. At a Berklee audition, if you're a "shredder," play some kickin' piece in that bag. You'll sound more comfortable and excel musically doing your thing! It's really kind of ridiculous to hear a guy who's obviously a metal player hackin' through a chord-melody arrangement of "Autumn Leaves" because he *thought* he was *supposed* to play a jazz piece.

Remember though, that's *if* you have the option of choosing. Many schools with contemporary music programs still want to hear straight-ahead jazz pieces, and sometimes even classical pieces during an audition. If you can do both, that's great, but if the proposed pieces are just too far away from your normal musical scope, you're either going to have to get that stuff together (which could be a good learning experience) or you're going to have to ask yourself if the school is really a good "fit" for you.

IF YOU'RE USING A PLAY-ALONG, BRING A BACKUP.

Sometimes schools provide a live band for auditionees, sometimes just a couple of faculty jump in and play, but many auditions can be done to a play-along recording. This can be a good choice if you're playing rock, metal, or other high-energy styles where just a backing keyboard or second guitar might be a little lackluster. Also, auditions are generally short in duration, so trying to get a complicated arrangement together in short time is usually not a good idea. If you are permitted to perform with a prerecorded source, make sure that you have it backed up. This can include an extra CD or your own media player (MP3 player, laptop, etc.). Occasionally, an applicant will bring his or her own band, but check for clearance on this, and whether a drum set, bass amp, etc. is available for the band's use. Don't forget that playing a solo piece is usually a viable solution, which could include jazz chord solos, traditional classical pieces, and any number of ideas that show off your musicality in a good light. At Berklee, arrangements can and should feature improvisation as part of the performance. It's also typical to improvise on blues with the adjudicators.

RULE NUMBER ONE AGAIN: COME PREPARED!

Plan to arrive early, warm up, and be ready to go at your appointed time. Things happen while traveling, but do your best to be punctual. It helps to relax you for your performance and keeps the audition team on time. Try to keep setup of pedals and the like to a minimum. Tune your axe before you enter the audition space. While it's crucial to play in tune at an audition (this is typical evaluation criterion), don't pull out the instrument cold from the case and then tune. Feel free to tweak the tuning throughout the audition. But, it's really amazing to see how much time gets wasted in auditions due to radical tuning adjustments and too much stuff to set up. That being said, do make sure you have an instrument cable, picks, music, or whatever you need to play your audition (like your play-along recording), and *check* your tuning (quickly) before you begin! Some guitarists bring two instruments: one in standard tuning, the other perhaps in a drop tuning. A great time saver.

BE PREPARED TO SIGHT-READ.

Musicians read music to convey and understand musical ideas. Guitar is a difficult instrument to read on, to be sure! But guitarists who only read tab or plead ignorance when it comes to reading will be left in the dust. Modern music schools are looking for guitarists with highly developed musicianship skills, which include reading. There certainly have been great musicians who can't read a note, can't even tell you a chord name, and they will be some of the greatest players of all time! The ear is the greatest music skill you can develop. But schools are balancing musicians on all instruments to co-exist in ensembles, ear-training classes, etc. Guitarists who don't read have a harder time participating in these classes. It used to be, "Well the guy's a guitarist, what do you expect?" That lick doesn't cut it now. You can be the hottest guitarist on the planet on your own without being able to read, but when it comes to music school, you're a risk. Lack of good reading skills has become a liability when auditioning for professional music schools. Prepare, and start reading now!

PRACTICE "CALL AND RESPONSE" FOR BOTH PITCH PLAYBACK AND RHYTHM PLAYBACK.

This is playing back phrases by ear, identifying scales, arpeggios, and harmonic elements. This material can vary widely, so get a good handle on basic theory elements, and practice learning phrases by ear, and associating them with content on the fingerboard. This means if you hear a phrase from the harmonic-minor scale, you should be able to relate it to a logical fingering for playback on the guitar. Be prepared to sing and pitch-match. Sounds scary, if you don't sing, but believe me, you'll be singing in ear training class on day one, so get used to it! This is an evaluation of musicianship skills, which translates into aptitude for success in classes and as a professional musician. See the ear training exercises in appendix C.

RECAP

- Find out what's expected of you in an audition by a particular school.

- Prepare your audition material following the guidelines dictated by the school.

- Choose your pieces to display what you do best, following directives for specific content.

- In addition to playing your audition piece, be prepared to improvise on a blues progression or on standard chord progressions. It helps to have prepared some typical jazz standards like "All the Things You Are," "Stella by Starlight," or "Autumn Leaves," for example. Having some jazz heads together like "Oleo," "Au Privave," or "Donna Lee" is smart, too. These are "universal" tunes that practically every good jazz player knows. They might be spontaneously incorporated into your audition.

- Arrive on time, tuned, and ready to play. Avoid long setup times like the plague!

- In addition to your instrumental skills, practice musicianship skills: reading, ear training, and theory, to display your "overall" aptitude for admission.

BONUS ADVICE

- Leave bad attitude at the door! Arrogance, sarcastic comments, and ego-driven smart-assed quips don't impress adjudicators. It only reflects on the applicant in a negative way. Be cooperative, gracious, and grateful for the time afforded you during your audition.

- Scholarships are won by the applicants who do all the above in a superior way. Make sure to read the interview with Berklee's Damien Bracken in appendix B.

- Many schools have instituted a policy of requesting a pre-audition "screening" recording or DVD to weed out unsuitable applicants. Once again, pay attention to specific requirements. Obviously, while a "pro" studio filming isn't always possible, turn in the best quality you can afford to gain a chance to audition "live."

- Have fun, and try to enjoy yourself in the audition process. Try to project who you are honestly, without putting on "airs." If at first you don't succeed… try again!

A Listening Guide to Jazz Guitar

Listening to diverse jazz guitar players is helpful, stylistically. It's a good thing to have a sense of the guitar's role in jazz history for comping ideas as well as soloing concepts. Start with Eddie Lang in the 1920s, then check out the big band rhythm players in the 1930s like Freddie Green and Allen Reuss. There's also some great duo guitar playing by Dick McDonough and Karl Kress. Guitarist George Van Eps is a study in himself and a very influential guitar educator!

Django Reinhardt with his Hot Club of France group was a hotbed of great guitar playing. Eventually, Django would play electric guitar, became one of the greatest guitar stylists of all time, and was very influential on guitarists, from Les Paul right up to the present. By the late 1930s/early 1940s, there was a shift to smaller jazz groups featuring electric guitar, and the king here is Charlie Christian, the most influential jazz guitarist of his generation. His accomplishments fathered players like Irving Asby, Oscar Moore, Jimmy Wyble, Wes Montgomery, Joe Pass, Jim Hall, Grant Green, Barney Kessel, Kenny Burrell, Tal Farlow, Jimmy Raney, Herb Ellis, Mundell Lowe, Sal Salvador, Billy Bauer, Barry Galbraith, Bucky Pizzarelli, George Barnes, Johnny Smith, Howard Roberts, Chuck Wayne, Tony Motolla, Joe Negri, Cal Collins, Bob Bain, Ted Dunbar, Ray Crawford, and many others. By the late 1940s and 1950s, the electric guitar was ubiquitous! The guitarists just mentioned were all active in jazz and the music industry in general. They traveled and performed in clubs, on stage in concerts, and in pit orchestras, and several of these guys worked in the studios on "commercial" recordings, on film soundtracks, and on television shows. Later, many also became jazz guitar educators, produced books on jazz guitar, conducted clinics, and took positions at universities and colleges teaching guitar.

The 1960s saw the addition of the nylon-string guitar with the bossa nova explosion in the United States. Brazilian players using nylon-string guitars like Laurindo Almedia, Baden Powell, and Joao Gilberto had a huge impact on jazz guitar and the incorporation of Brazilian rhythms in comping. Many Brazilian tunes were integrated into the jazz guitarist's repertoire.

The next generation of great jazz guitarists was coming up. Pat Martino and George Benson started as mainstream players, but diversified their talents as the fusion of jazz and rock was happening in the late 1960s. Lenny Breau came from a country music background and was a protégé of Chet Atkins. Groups like Miles Davis' units and Chick Corea's Return to Forever fostered the talents of players like John McLaughlin, Bill Conners, and Al Di Meola. Boston and the Berklee College of Music was an epicenter of guitaristic development. In addition to Al Di Meola, other famous jazz guitarists associated with Berklee (and/or living in Boston) included Mick Goodrick, Larry Coryell, John Abercrombie, Mike Stern, John Scofield, Bill Frisell, Pat Metheny, and others. Around this time, there were many extraordinary guitarists active in New York City, among them Gene Bertoncini, Jack Wilkins, Vic Juris, and Rodney Jones. Later in the 1980s, players based in Los Angeles like Scott Henderson, Frank Gambale, and Larry Carlton forged their own fusion jazz styles.

This quick timeline will take you through the millennia. One of the things that I find especially wonderful about all the players on the timeline (which is woefully inadequate and omits many important guitarists) is the concurrent activities of all these players. Some pushed the boundaries of style and technique, some kept tradition alive, some were just gigging to make a living, but they all were making great music. Since 2000, innovative developments have been happening all over the planet with the latest generation of jazz guitarists. Today's younger players respect and emulate these master players and continue growing the tradition of jazz guitar values with imagination and performance.

Try to keep your mind open, listen, get out there, and play!

Chord Voicings

Here are some basic drop-2 and drop-3 voicings, and some offshoot voicings with tensions. Many of these voicings incorporate usable tensions added to or subbed for low-degree chord tones. This is just a partial list of possibilities of some particularly user-friendly "grips" and some forms that grow out of a "master" chord fingering. The "plain" seventh chord on the first example is the "master" form. Many of these examples grow from a master form. Strings on the grids with no dots (X) are to be muted or omitted from the chord; those marked with 0 are to be played open. All examples are built on the pitch C. Find the root in the chord and transpose to all other pitches. Chords that use a 9th instead of a root need to be "reckoned" from another chord tone. A circled number indicates the strings on which the low note of the chord is played.

You'll notice that this small appendix is not as large as many of your typical commercial guitar chord books. The main reason for this is that I've reduced the chord structures down to the three primary chord colors: major 7, minor 7, and dominant, with an emphasis on dominant 7 structures. My thinking here is to have you find the other 7th chord types (7♭5, 7♯5, Maj7♯5, etc.) by altering the basic chord shapes presented here. So, if you need to find a 7♯5 grip, pick one of the dominant 7 voicings and raise the 5th! This a more "organic" way to get your chords together, because you create a new voicing from something you already know. It's recycling! Good for your mind and less trees used to present page after page of guitar hieroglyphs! That said, a chord dictionary I recommend is Rick Peckham's *Berklee Jazz Guitar Chord Dictionary* (Berklee Press, 2007).

I'll talk a little later about naming pitches in chords as tensions vs. low degrees.

DOMINANT 7 VOICINGS

Drop-2 Middle String Set

Basic drop-2 voicings always "lay" over four adjacent strings. "String sets" can be designated as top, middle, and lower groups (sets) of four strings each. Generally, the middle and top string sets usually sound clearest, and the bottom set tends to be a little muddy.

Fig. A.1. Dominant 7 Voicings in Drop-2 Middle String Set

Drop-2 Voicings on the Top String Set

Here are more drop-2 voicings, but on the top string set. Notice that we're starting to repeat the same notes on different string groups, and sometimes even on the same strings. You might have noticed that many of these C7 chord shapes function as F#7 structures as well. Dominant 7 chords have a built-in tritonic relationship between two chords—in this case, C7 and F#7. These chords share the same guide tones, and the roots are a tritone apart. Generally speaking, one chord will have an "inside" quality, and the other will be more "outgoing" in nature. Can you identify the chord scales that relate to these voicings?

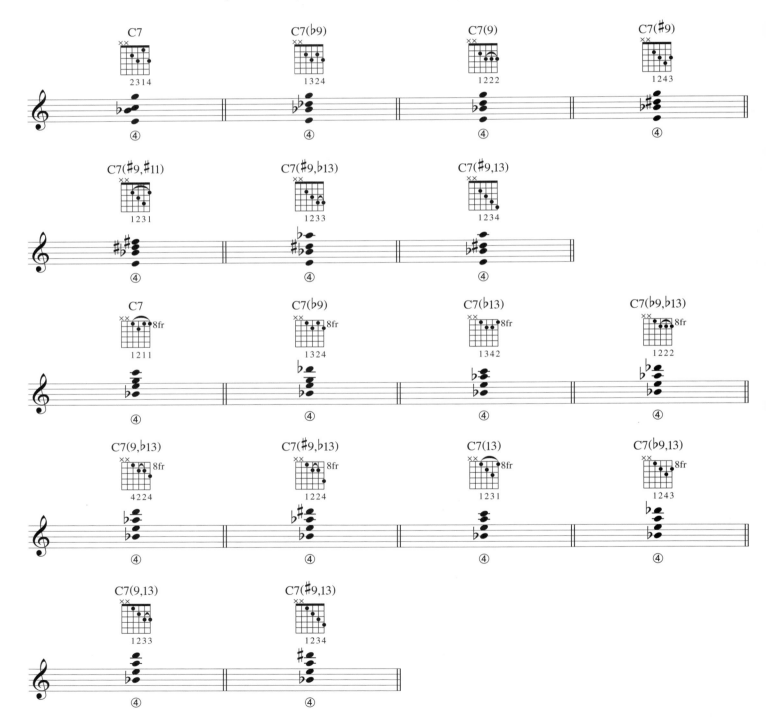

Fig. A.2. Dominant 7 in Drop-2 Voicings on the Top String Set

Drop-3 Voicings and Variants

Here are some drop-3 voicings of dominant 7 and some derivatives. On the first example of C7 (figure A.3), many guitarists delete the 5 and double the root to give us the variation in voicing 2. While not strictly a drop-3 (bastard drop 3?), this is a widely used voicing. Tension substitutions can be utilized on both, but these examples come from the doubled-root version. Try both the doubled root and reinstalling the 5 as the low note too!

Notice that some of these voicings contain the root as well as a 9, ♯9, and sometimes a ♭9. These are very typical voicings, but some theory situations frown upon a ♭9 interval in the voicings as you would find in the first C7♭9 example. Once again, use your ears. It's a matter of judgment; you make the call!

One other thing to call our attention to: the naming of ♭13 vs. ♯5 and ♭5 vs. ♯11. We guitarists (having so few fingers to create voicings with) tend to interchange these chords freely. And as long as things sound good, that's all that matters. Technically speaking, though, a ♭13 is truly a ♭13 and not a ♯5 when it co-exists with the natural 5 of the genesis scale (such as Mixolydian ♭6, the fifth mode of the melodic-minor scale). Same thing with the ♯11 vs. ♭5 (as in the Lydian ♭7 scale). Both of these scale examples contain a natural 5, which *could* be incorporated into a voicing. If the scale contains a ♯5 or ♭5, then you're dealing with a 7♯5 or 7♭5 chord, *technically*. Ears open!

While all the examples so far have been four-note chords, we can add other available tensions and chord tones by utilizing the first string and expand to five-note voicings. (Check out the second and third line in the next example.)

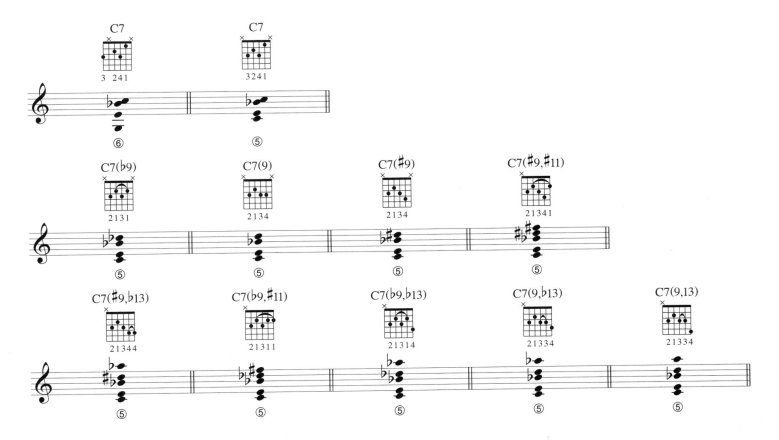

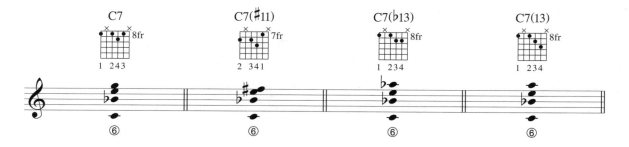

Fig. A.3. Drop-3 Voicings of Dominant 7 (and Derivatives)

Drop-3 voicings can be played with the top note on the first string as well as the second string. Try some of the previous four-note examples with the top note on the high "E" string. Transpose by octave, where necessary.

More Voicings with Root and 9

This drop-3 chord shape can also utilize the top string to add more tensions (sometimes doubling the root) and create more variations.

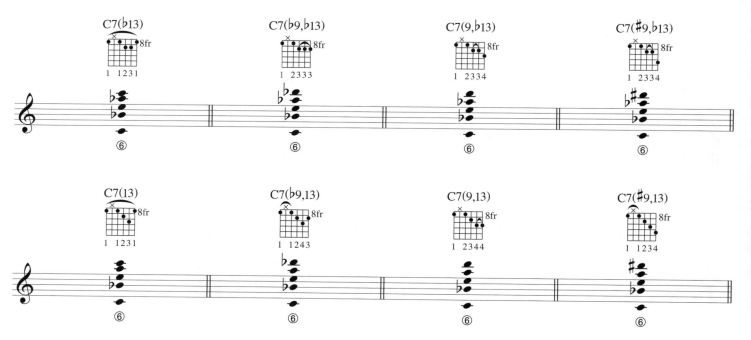

Fig. A.4. More Voicings with Root, 9, and/or 13

DOMINANT 7SUS4 VOICINGS

Here are some 7sus4 voicings. The chord scale producing these structures can be Mixolydian, Phrygian, Phrygian major, harmonic minor, etc.

The bottom row features some bigger voicings utilizing T10 (tension 10).

Play around with these, and look for other combinations of 7sus4 with tensions.

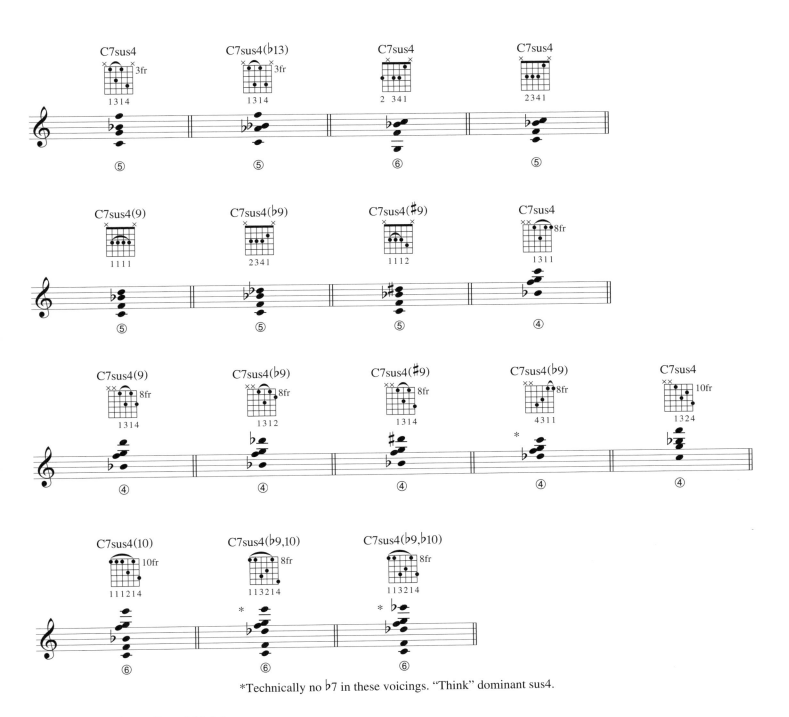

*Technically no ♭7 in these voicings. "Think" dominant sus4.

Fig. A.5. Dominant 7sus4 Voicings

MAJOR 7 CHORD VOICINGS

Drop-2 Voicings

Let's move on to some major chord forms. Many can be derived from the previous dominant forms. After getting the hang of some of these, try them again, but with the fifth of the chord raised or lowered. This gives us the Maj7♭5 and Maj7♯5 chord types. Some of the new grips will be uncomfortable—in some cases, impossible—for you to play, so give those the big X! Play what sounds and feels good!

*In the last three voicings, notice that there's a 9 on the bottom of the voicing. They're high enough to sound okay.

Fig. A.6. Major Chord Voicings

Drop-3 Voicings and Variants

Here are some drop-3 variations of Maj7. Like the previous dominant 7 versions, the "pure" drop-3 voicing in the second example has been "bastardized" into the doubled root version. In the last two, I named the tensions as low degree numbers: 13 is 6 and 2 is 9. As with the previous dominant 7 drop 3s, try some of these with the top note on the high E string. There's nothing like experience to see what works and what *doesn't* work.

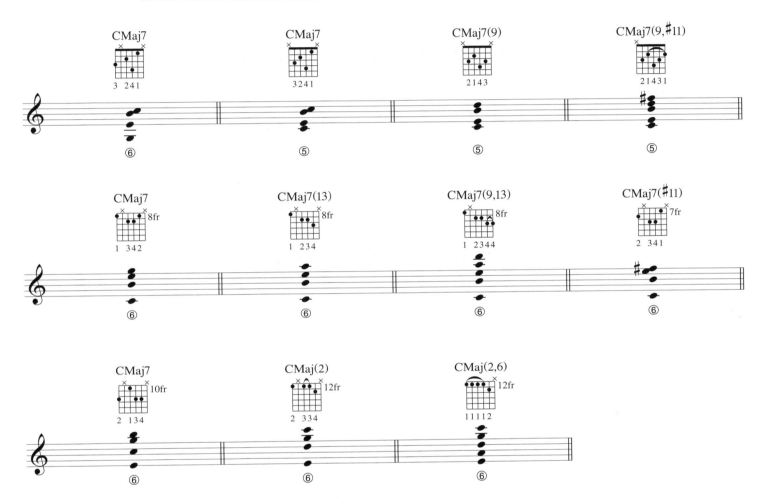

Fig. A.7. Drop-3 Voicings and Variants

MINOR 7 CHORD VOICINGS

Here are some minor 7 chord voicings. In voicings 3 and 4, the 11 could have been designated as a 4. Are you noticing that some previously presented 7sus4 chords are being presented as minor 7(11)? Which are drop-2 and which are drop-3? Again, some voicings have more than four notes.

Fig. A.8. Minor Chord Voicings

DIMINISHED CHORD VOICINGS

The first line shows the four "classic" diminished chord shapes on the guitar.

Fig. A.9. Diminished Chord Voicings

Basically, when viewing a diminished scale, the eight notes can be broken down into the four chord tones of the basic diminished 7 chord (like C°7) and four tension tones that themselves form another diminished 7 chord (D°7). A tension tone can replace any low degree of the "basic" four-tone diminished 7 chord. A tension can also be added to the basic diminished 7 chord, as your fingers allow. There are many more diminished-oriented chords, but they function more in the category of dominant 7 with tensions.

Once again, just to recap, many of the other seventh chord types, such as major 7♯5, major 7♭5, minor/major 7, minor 7♭5, 7♭5, and 7♯5 are missing from these fingerings. They can be created by simply applying that chord's formula to the dominant, major, and minor structures given here. All these examples are in C major, C minor, and C dominant, so the 3rd is always an E or E♭, the 5th is G♭ (♭5), G natural (natural 5), or G♯ (♯5), and the 7th is ♭7 (B♭) or natural 7 (B natural). In other words, you can create a chord structure such as minor 7♭5 by altering the 5th of one of the "plain" minor 7 fingerings; it's the same with the major 7 and dominant 7th variations. In fact, this is a good way to memorize new structures and apply music theory at the same time. It's easier to learn new chords when you can "see" their derivation from a chord you know.

Usually, the dominant 7(♯11) can be thought of as 7♭5, and 7(♭13) can be thought of as ♯5. Any of the dominant 7 chords can move the given 5th up or down a half step to create 7♭5 and 7♯5. Let you ear guide your choices! Some fingerings may be prohibitive or even impossible for you. Retain the ones that work.

APPENDIX B

Interview with Damien Bracken on Scholarships/Auditioning

What makes Berklee's system unique in terms of colleges that audition for music majors?

I think one thing that's unique to Berklee is the kind of breadth of the kind of student that we're looking for. So while a particular kind of conservatory might be looking for the lead trombone chair for their big band, Berklee might be looking for that, but also a whole slew of other things, such as students who are focused more on music business, focused more on music therapy, focused perhaps on composition.

So it's a widely diversified pool of applicants that are coming in.

Correct. And the approach that Berklee takes to its admissions process is really a very holistic one. We look at every aspect of the student's application, not just the audition. The audition is certainly important. I think equally important is the interview that takes place.

How can prospective students prepare for an interview?

A little bit of self-examination. On the application for admission, there are fourteen questions that we ask students to respond to. The responses to those questions are the basis for the interview, so those questions range from everything from "What's your practice routine?" to "How do you manage your time as a high school student and a student musician, and perhaps performing in different bands in your neighborhood?" and things like that.

Back to the audition. You find a lot of people coming in kind of acting like deer in the headlights. Some guys are really well prepared, others are playing a piece of music at an audition because a teacher told them it's a jazz school and they should be doing jazz pieces, even though the guy's a metal player! Many applicants don't know what to prepare and what the audition process involves. And a lot of folks spend audition time tuning their guitar, which should have been tuned pre-audition, or spend five minutes setting up pedals.

Right…. exactly. You see that a lot.

So, I want to make things really clear. Applicants should know how to prepare for the requirements of a particular school, and that they should research what the procedure is and what the school is looking for in a potential student before they do the audition and the interview. This includes stylistically wide-ranging audition material as long as said material fits into guidelines outlined by a school. Right?

Yes, and I think the stylistic diversity issue is one that again is kind of unique to Berklee. We don't dictate to students a repertoire. We don't say, "Choose this particular list of audition pieces." So in some senses it's a leap of faith for the students, because they may have a teacher saying, "It's a jazz school, prepare 'Autumn Leaves.'" Whereas their true love is heavy metal or some other style of music, or they may be a singer/songwriter that's doing a lot of creative stuff on their own.

For sure.

We are asking for a lot of the applicant, but we are telling the applicant that if they don't show us who they truly are as a musician, it won't serve them well in the application process.

That's a good thing to be thinking about when you come in, representing yourself honestly as a musician within the auditions framework. Do you have any general advice on what makes the difference between the players that get scholarship monies, and those that don't? Like, what comes across about an applicant, in an audition transcript and in the interview, that most informs the decision regarding scholarship awards?

Definitely critical is a preparedness—a kind of confidence, and familiarity with the material that you are presenting to the audition team. We outline for the students the various aspects that will be presented to them in the audition. There is a lot of material on the website to help them practice for the audition; vamps, and play-alongs, and things like that.

Even some of the minor things, like you were saying, in terms of tuning your guitar before you walk into the room, being ready to play. Berklee's audition is 15 minutes, but it's the fastest 15 minutes of your life! It goes by….

What you are actually saying here is that you are awarding scholarships to people who are taking care of business. In addition to playing well, they have their act together. They're coming in prepared. They have a focus.

They've practiced the material. They have a focus.

That translates into the personification of what you are looking for in a Berklee student, beyond instrumental skills.

One of the very simple questions we ask students in the interview is, "Why are you choosing Berklee? Why is it that you want to come to Berklee?" And I think as simple as that question sounds, it's critically important. If you are searching for a music college program, you're going to spend four years of your life developing your skills and spending a lot of money on attending college. You'd better know that you've chosen the right college to suit your needs and your outcomes, so do a lot of research in advance. Research what kind of faculty are at the college. Talk to your instructors and your family about what kind of career track you want to take in music, and what kind of curriculum would serve that best. And be prepared to answer those kinds of questions, not just to the interview team, but sometimes it's asked in the audition as well. "What do you plan on studying at Berklee?" Know the answer to that question, and know why.

Some people audition more than once, either because a previous audition didn't go so well and they wanted to do a better shot, or they're trying to get maybe a better scholarship award. What are your thoughts on that? What makes a difference when you see a person coming back again? And what do you look for in the new transcripts to be able to make a decision that this person has moved closer to that goal, of either attaining more scholarship, or getting it in the first place?

Again, it all tends to boil down to the level of preparedness for the audition. We have all of these different kinds of students coming to us with different kinds of strengths, so what makes the difference in terms of whether you get an $8,000 scholarship or a $12,000 scholarship?

Being prepared, and being focused. Confidence is a really huge thing. When a student performs a piece that their teacher recommended because of a perception of what kind of program we might have at Berklee, when in actual fact, the student would be better served performing a piece of music that they know really well—that they can perform really well, that they really believe in, that they really feel the music when they play it—that's a better choice.

Be yourself musically.

Be yourself. And you know, that's a leap of faith.

That's a big departure from a lot of schools that require say, classic bebop pieces as audition vehicles. Some places, they'll even dictate choices between three or four selections within a category, like a bop tune, or a modal tune, sometimes by jazz period, so this Berklee audition is really kind of wide-ranging. That also allows for a lot of diversity in the applicant, not only to be a good instrumentalist, but maybe be a talented composer as well, or possibly someone who's recording and interested in the technology aspect of music, or music business.

That's exactly right. There are so many different avenues now for students to approach music. Students are learning music through their computer, through their laptop, on the Web. You can jam online with people all around the world. So it's not so much, it's not necessary that students will come to us with a traditional background. We have a lot of musicians audition at Berklee who are essentially self-taught and are huge talents. We admit them and award them scholarships.

When a person comes in with another kind of discipline other than just the instrumental skills, should they be bringing support materials, scores, recordings, and any kind of documentation of their other musical interests or specialties? [Note: Every Berklee applicant does an instrumental audition.]

Yes. That material is looked at in the interview. We also ask students to point us to a website (Facebook, MySpace, YouTube, etc.), so that when it's time for the Board of Admissions to go into committee, we can refer to material. That's very common now.

That's a great thing to be able to include in terms of support materials.

Yes, exactly. Because all the students are doing production with their bands. They're going into their home recording studio and doing demos and things like that. We want to see if you are interested in music, how are you engaging in music, what are you doing.

Ultimately, how do you make the decision about who gets into Berklee?

When we think about the admissions process to Berklee, we boil it down to two essential questions. The first question the Board of Admissions has to answer for every applicant is, is this student ready? This question might apply to their readiness in terms of the preparation on their instrument, their knowledge of the instrument, their demonstrated craft on the instrument, but it also speaks to their level of preparedness in terms of the research that they have done about Berklee, the reason why they are choosing Berklee, why they feel that Berklee program is the best fit for them. And it also speaks to a certain level of maturity in the applicant, or a clarity in that applicant, that this is somebody who is well-informed, well-prepared, and if admitted to Berklee, will be a good fit for the college.

If we can answer that in the positive, the other question that we ask is, what will they bring? So we are looking at a school here of 4,000 students, and we'll have approximately 1,000 students in the entering class. We'll have close to 5,000 students applying for that entering class, so what is it about the 1,000 that matriculate to Berklee that will bring the Berklee community up another notch? What are they going to contribute? That's ultimately how we make our admissions decisions.

Ear Training Exercises

Listen to each example, then repeat it back. Following each example, if you need more time before repeating the phrase, pause the CD.

MELODIC CALL AND RESPONSE

Melodic Call and Response 1

Track 77

Melodic Call and Response 2

Melodic Call and Response 3

Melodic Call and Response 4

Melodic Call and Response 5

Melodic Call and Response 6

Melodic Call and Response 7

Track 78

Melodic Call and Response 8

Melodic Call and Response 9

Melodic Call and Response 10

Melodic Call and Response 11

Track 79

Melodic Call and Response 12

Melodic Call and Response 13

Melodic Call and Response 14

Melodic Call and Response 15

Melodic Call and Response 16

Track 80

Melodic Call and Response 17

Melodic Call and Response 18

Melodic Call and Response 19

Melodic Call and Response 20

Melodic Call and Response 21

Melodic Call and Response 22

Track 81

Melodic Call and Response 23

Melodic Call and Response 24

Melodic Call and Response 25

RHYTHMIC CALL AND RESPONSE

Examples 1 to 12 are straight-eighth 2-bar phrases. Following each example, if you need more time before repeating the phrase, pause the CD.

Track 82

Rhythmic Call and Response 1

Rhythmic Call and Response 2

Rhythmic Call and Response 3

Rhythmic Call and Response 4

Rhythmic Call and Response 5

Rhythmic Call and Response 6

Rhythmic Call and Response 7

Rhythmic Call and Response 8

Rhythmic Call and Response 9

Rhythmic Call and Response 10

Rhythmic Call and Response 11

Rhythmic Call and Response 12

For examples 13 to 25, listen to each phrase on the CD and then repeat the rhythms in each bar. Swing through these twenty 4-bar phrases.

Track 83

Rhythmic Call and Response 13

Rhythmic Call and Response 14

Rhythmic Call and Response 15

Rhythmic Call and Response 16

Rhythmic Call and Response 17

Rhythmic Call and Response 18

Rhythmic Call and Response 19

Rhythmic Call and Response 20

Rhythmic Call and Response 21

Rhythmic Call and Response 22

Rhythmic Call and Response 23

Rhythmic Call and Response 24

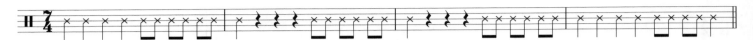

Rhythmic Call and Response 25

ABOUT THE AUTHOR

Mark White is a guitarist, composer, and producer. He has performed with the Boston Pops under Keith Lockhart, the Boston Musica Viva under Richard Pitman, the New England Ragtime Ensemble under Gunther Schuller, the Empire Brass Quintet, George Russell, Gil Evans, Anthony Braxton, the Kenny Hadley Big Band, the John Allmark Big Band, Victor Mendoza, Bernadette Peters, numerous theater engagements with touring Broadway companies including *City of Angels*, *Fiddler on the Roof*, *Annie*, and *A Chorus Line*, at the world premier and ensuing fifty performances of Phillip Glass's *The Fall of the House of Usher*, and many others. Festival performances include the Nuit Bleu and Nuit Black festivals in Quebec, Canada; the

Photo by Judah Chivian

Mare de Agosto Festival, Portugal; the Umbria Jazz Festival, Perugia, Italy; Settembre Musicale Festival, Torino, Italy; the San Juan Heineken Festival, Puerto Rico; the Seoul Jazz Festival, Seoul, Korea; the Tokyo Music Joy Festival, Tokyo, Japan; the Phoenix Jazz Festival, Kobe, Japan; and the Jazz Jamboree, Warsaw, Poland. He has toured the continental United States extensively, as well as Russia, Italy, Austria, and Slovenia.

Mark has performed clinics for Berklee College of Music in Ecuador, Italy, Japan, Korea, Mexico, Germany, Costa Rica, Spain, and Los Angeles. He has acted as a musical ambassador for the USIA in Bogata, Columbia, directing the Taller Jazz Nationale Jazz Workshop on two occasions. He is currently a senior professor of guitar at Berklee and is an active member of Berklee's A&I audition team. In addition to his duties at Berklee, Mark also teaches at the Commonwealth School in Boston and is staff guitarist for the ACME Rhythm Section, which backs productions for the Franklin School for the Performing Arts and New England Center for the Performing Arts.

White has recorded and produced the CD *Tunch* on the MMC label, two CDs with the group Last Trip: *Up with da Funk* and *Born Yesterday* on Grescotmar LTD, and has participated on numerous freelance studio projects. His compositions and arrangements have been performed and recorded by George Russell's Living Time Orchestra and by Kenny Burrell. He is the author of *Advanced Reading Etudes for Guitar* published by Grescotmar, and is a BMI Music Publisher (Whitmark Music Publishing). He holds a bachelor's and a master's degree from New England Conservatory.

INDEX